HOW WOMEN MAKE MONEY

JULIE V. WATSON

HOW WOMEN
MAKE MONEY

Inspirational Stories and
Practical Advice from Successful
Canadian Entrepreneurs

THE DUNDURN GROUP
TORONTO

Copy-Editor: Andrea Pruss
Design: Jennifer Scott
Printer: Transcontinental

National Library of Canada Cataloguing in Publication Data

Watson, Julie V., 1943-
How women make money : inspirational stories and practical advice from successful Canadian entrepreneurs/
    Julie V. Watson.

ISBN 1-55002-493-0

1. Businesswomen — Canada. 2. Women-owned business enterprises — Canada. 3. Entrepreneurship —Canada.
I. Title.

HD6099.W38 2004   338'.04'082   C2004-900461-1

1   2   3   4   5   08   07   06   05   04

Conseil des Arts du Canada **Canada Council for the Arts** Canada ONTARIO ARTS COUNCIL CONSEIL DES ARTS DE L'ONTARIO

We acknowledge the support of the **Canada Council for the Arts** and the **Ontario Arts Council** for our publishing program. We also acknowledge the financial support of the **Government of Canada** through the **Book Publishing Industry Development Program** and **The Association for the Export of Canadian Books**, and the **Government of Ontario** through the **Ontario Book Publishers Tax Credit** program, and the **Ontario Media Development Corporation's Ontario Book Initiative**.

Care has been taken to trace the ownership of copyright material used in this book. The author and the publisher welcome any information enabling them to rectify any references or credit in subsequent editions.
                                                              J. Kirk Howard, President

Printed and bound in Canada.
Printed on recycled paper.
www.dundurn.com

Dundurn Press
8 Market Street
Suite 200
Toronto, Ontario, Canada
M5E 1M6

Gazelle Book Services Limited
White Cross Mills
Hightown, Lancaster, England
LA1 4X5

Dundurn Press
2250 Military Road
Tonawanda NY
U.S.A. 14150

HOW WOMEN MAKE MONEY

Table of Contents

Introduction

Most of the people in your life are just passing through, the one whose opinion you have to really worry about is — you. The one who in the long run will look back and question, "Did I reach for my dreams, explore my potential, give it a good go?" The simple steps of exploring options and life choices will benefit your whole life, not just your career. By simply acknowledging your priorities — be they "significant other," children, career, or personal passions indulged — or best option a combination of all four — having a sense of what really matters to you is the first step to happiness and achievement.

Julie V. Watson

While I do believe we are in many ways a product of our early environment, I don't feel it creates a box from which there is no escape. Instead, our early years create a foundation — something to stand on while we build our own life.

We take the best to emulate, and the worst as an example of what not to do or be. Successful individuals, in both their personal and working lives, take lessons from their early experiences and build on them to create their own dreams — their own ideas of a good life.

I had the good fortune to be surrounded by women of strength and achievement when I was growing up. My mom, my grandmother, my aunts. Later on, my wonderful friends. These women were not so much entrepreneurs as achievers. They were, and are, women who took charge of their destiny and did something about making their way in life.

Family women all, they held jobs, had careers, were equal partners in taking financial responsibility for their families. While some of their marriages may not have come up to today's fairy-tale expectations, they lasted. My parents have been together sixty years and are still counting. These women made the best of what they had, enjoyed their lives, took pride in themselves and their accomplishments, and didn't give up.

My grandparents are gone now, but my grandmother will forever hold a place in my heart. She raised a large family. I always say it was a matriarchal family, for in her quiet way, she ruled. My grandfather, a lovely man adored by us all, quietly went about earning money and doing the man things around the house: fixing, building, gardening, I even remember him killing a chicken for supper.

He was a considerate, kind, caring man who first and foremost listened and who thought all of us grandkids wonderful. As importantly, he respected his girls as much as any man. For that one thing I thank my grandfather, my father, and my uncles. These men were not perfect, but they did treat women with basic respect and, for the most part, as equal partners, which went a long way toward instilling a sense of self-worth in my generation.

It is my firm belief that because the individuals in my family were raised with respect — taught both to give it and to expect it in return — the women I was surrounded by always approached the world as an equal and in return were treated that way. It's all in attitude.

If you lie down to be walked on, you will be treated as a door-mat. If you stand with pride, you will be counted and treated as one of the players.

So, too, do the rules of giving back apply. What you give out, the help you give to others, comes back.

One of my earliest memories is of my grandfather shaking up cream to make a bit of butter as a special treat for my grandmother. This was just after World War II, when such things were luxuries. A cabinetmaker, he left a legacy of furniture, trays, and jewellery boxes, as well as many good memories. Yet for all those memories of him, Nanny was the stronger presence — the one who influenced me the most.

She, more than anyone else, taught me the concept of making do, of seeing the best in a situation and running with that rather than dwelling on the negative. By example she showed me that you could do extra special things with few or no resources. Take Christmas. As soon as the air turned from sultry to crisp she would begin making little treasures, buying small treats. Every grandchild was always remembered with a wee gift, no matter how tight money. And each was thoughtfully chosen for the individual. One of the best I remember getting at Christmas was a wee doll complete with clothes and a tiny blanket and pillow. It would all fit in a small box, easy for a little girl to carry. Important for a child whose parents treated her as an extension of themselves and took her everywhere possible. I remember a chest of drawers made of matchboxes, cradles from six-quart baskets. Hand-sewn pencil cases with treasured coloured pencils. She made my toddler son a lovely "English" winter hat and coat from an out-of-fashion coat of her own.

As the oldest grandchild, it was deemed important that I have a big wedding. I was not averse to such a thing, but money was a major issue — we didn't have any. In stepped my mother and grandmother. Now Mom was working full-time, yet she made my wedding dress. She and my dad made my wedding cake. Nanny sewed dresses for the bridesmaids and flower girl, along with headpieces — created from a strip of cardboard fixed into a circle, covered with the satin of the dresses, and enhanced with tulle. She made my going away suit and my trousseau. And she took me by the hand, went out, and purchased unbleached sheeting, which we turned into wonderful bedding. I have those sheets today, and forty years later they are still some of the best to sleep in. If only she were around to help me make them fitted! The biggest expense at our wedding was the photographer, whom Nanny insisted we hire. She demanded a photo of our Canadian family — some thirty people — directing the operation to her standards of proper placing of individuals. We all treasure that image.

Nanny didn't hold down an outside job. Yet she *always* worked. She constantly made things. She sewed, she knit, and she crocheted beautiful things — coats, shawls, tablecloths, placemats — earning her "pin money." She baked, pickled, sewed ... the list is endless.

My parents and I were the first to immigrate to Canada, followed in quick succession by Mom's parents, her sisters and their families, friends.

Many stayed with those who had arrived before until moms and dads found jobs and got established. So too, many of us stayed with my grandparents while in transition between homes, jobs, or, in my case, schools.

The women in my family were not super women, or super moms; they were, and are, simply familiar with getting on with it and making the best they could out of what they had. And they are not unique, nor alone. There are thousands just like them out there ready to stand as role models any time we ask them.

There are so many women, not CEOs, not founders of big companies, just women in the trenches, trying to do their best for their families, their communities. I'm one of that army of women who wear hundreds of different hats every day. And I'm prouder of that than of just about anything else in my life.

The examples of women to take pride in are legion. The lessons to be learned from their experience and advice are even greater.

This book is not meant to be a workbook, but rather a glimpse of the achievements of great Canadian women, with their advice and some how-to help to round it out. In the following pages we will look at women working in many sectors. While a particular section of the book may not apply directly to you, or to the field in which you are interested, I do urge you to read the stories of what all of these women do, how they got where they are, and their advice. It's an uplifting experience.

Our focus is women pursuing their dreams and passions to develop businesses of their own. We must begin by revealing who we are talking to with this book. First and foremost it is to the self-employed, the small business owner. Much of what you will find between these covers will inspire and be useful to anyone seeking independence and growth through marketing skills that they have. I do not advocate this work as being an instruction book for those seeking to develop a large company, although it can't hurt. Rather, I hope it will help inspire those aspiring to earn their own money, their own way.

What we do is acknowledge that success for many, many women is not measured as government officials seem wont to do, by large cash flow, by numbers of employees, by becoming a mega-size exporter.

Instead we measure success as attaining the goals that the individual woman is pursuing. For many that is supplementing income, while other things in life are a primary focus (children and spouses, medical concerns, aging parents, education, etc.). For others it may be generating their own income while enjoying a lifestyle of their choosing. Seniors may simply need to supplement their pensions, hobbyists to fund their recreational pursuits.

A friend who proofread this manuscript commented that the amount of information, the number of stories contained between these covers, is almost overwhelming. It's true, and I've barely scratched the surface. So my request to you is that you treat this book as one you come back to time and time again.

According to Stats Canada, women are now starting businesses at twice the rate of men, with women starting half of all new businesses. Women own one-third of small and medium-size businesses in Canada.

Then of course we have some women who are seriously building a business: the women who are the models for others to follow. The stars. We have not given as much space to the sheer number of super achievers as we could have, simply because there are so many star-status entrepreneurial women that we would not have room left for all the things I want to include. There is also the fact that the award winners tend to get a lot of publicity, so you will have read about them elsewhere.

While we have tried to include all regions of the country in our profiles, it is naturally stronger in the areas that I am most familiar with: the Maritimes, where I live; Ontario, where I grew up; and British Columbia and Alberta, where family resides.

In fact, I could have written the whole book using examples of women doing great things from my home province of Prince Edward Island. Even with a population smaller than most Canadian cities, "the Island" is representative of Canada in that we have an active, vibrant segment of women working in a wide and diverse range of businesses.

I have not begun to list all of the diverse opportunities out there. There are far too many to try. Instead, I have focused on those I know. Read them all, and see how each woman has reached the goals she defined for herself. Then think about how the emerging patterns can affect your thinking and your life.

Of all of the sections in this book, the most important is the chapter on planning. Please read it carefully. Try using our forms, or at least follow the concept of detailing your goals and aspirations, your life realities, and your achievements. You will probably work out your own personalized version that works better for you, and that is a good thing. Our purpose is to set you on the right path to your destination, and to have you acknowledge all of the positive steps that you have taken along the way.

I do urge you to read all chapters even though the subject may not seem to apply to you. The decision of how to break down the information was a difficult one, and remains that way even now as I complete the manuscript. There are many examples of achieving women, many bits of advice that cross over from section to section. So do read them all.

The Power of Women

In late 2002, the prime minister of Canada announced the creation of the first Prime Minister's Task Force on Women Entrepreneurs to provide advice on how the federal government can enhance the contribution of women entrepreneurs to the Canadian economy. That report was released in late 2003, just as I was completing this book.

It offers an abundance of information about the challenges facing women. It also tells us that small business is the fastest-growing segment of the business sector in Canada and that women-owned businesses are the fastest-growing part of that segment, with women creating twice as many new businesses as men. It reports, "It is clear that Canadian women are creating a range of businesses that fall outside the traditional model of paid employment. Any definition of an 'entrepreneurial economy' must recognize this diverse range of activity — from one-person practices, to small businesses with a few employees, to large enterprises with many employees."

The significance of the contribution of entrepreneurial Canadian women to Canada's economy was first recognized in 1996 in the groundbreaking study *Myths and Realities: The Economic Power of Women-Led*

Firms in Canada. The research revealed that at that time there were over 700,000 women-led firms in Canada, providing 1.7 million jobs. It also revealed that the number of women-led firms was increasing at twice the national average. Unfortunately, in the absence of more recent research, these figures are still being quoted seven years later.

For this reason, the report from the Prime Minister's Task Force on Women Entrepreneurs is of vital importance to our future. First and

The Prime Minister's Task Force on Women Entrepreneurs offered up a "Summary of Salient Facts" that are indicative of just what a force women in business are:

- There are more than 821,000 women entrepreneurs in Canada.
- Canadian women entrepreneurs contribute in excess of $18.109 billion to the Canadian economy every year.
- Self-employment has grown faster in the past twenty-five years than paid employment.
- One in six workers in Canada is self-employed.
- Self-employment among women rose from 8.6 percent of workers in 1976 to 11.5 percent in 2002.
- Since 1976, the average annual growth rate of self-employment for women has been 5.3 percent, compared with 2.2 percent for men.
- The number of women entrepreneurs grew by 8 percent between 1996 and 2001, compared with a 0.6 percent increase for men.
- Between 1981 and 2001, the number of women entrepreneurs in Canada increased 208 percent, compared with a 38 percent increase for men.
- One-third of self-employed Canadians in 2002 were women.
- Women entrepreneurs held ownership in 45 percent of Canadian small and medium enterprises (SMEs) in 2000.
- Only 9 percent of women entrepreneurs are involved in international business.

- The likelihood of self-employment in women increases with age, and most are between the ages of thirty-five and fifty-four.
- Average earnings for women who are self-employed or work for their own account are lower than for employed women.
- Half of self-employed women work at home, thus showing the economic impact of home-based businesses.
- 60 percent of women entrepreneurs chose self-employment and would not prefer paid work.
- 78 percent of all self-employed individuals are voluntarily self-employed, with independence and freedom stated as the main reason for becoming self-employed.
- Women make up 40 percent of solo self-employed and just over one-quarter of employers.
- Women in Canada make up a larger share of the self-employed than in any other country.
- Only 17 percent of self-employed women make more than $30,000 a year, compared with 42 percent of men.
- Average annual sales are significantly lower for women-owned firms. In 2000, women-owned SMEs averaged $311,289 in annual sales, compared with $654,294 in sales for firms owned by men.
- In 2000, women held at least 50 percent ownership in 31 percent of knowledge-based industry (KBI) firms and 31 percent of manufacturing firms.
- Women tend to own firms in slower growth and higher risk sectors, such as retail and service, in which access to financing is relatively more challenging.
- Women-owned businesses are younger, with 28 percent having entered the market since 1996, compared with 23 percent of firms owned by men.
- Women make up 38 percent of the self-employed Aboriginal population.
- Between 1996 and 2001, the number of self-employed Aboriginal women increased by 58 percent, versus a 44 percent increase for men.

foremost, everyone should obtain a copy, read it, and use it as a lobbying tool with our government.

These two reports raise the profile of women entrepreneurs and heighten our expectations about both opportunity and the support we should be able to expect in starting and developing businesses.

There is great excitement, momentum, and a level of expectation encouraging women. It is up to us to maintain that by working with organizations and by having expectations for success.

The evidence is there. Women can, and do, build effective businesses that make profits and are important economic contributors. Whether you choose to join their ranks is up to you. I do hope that by telling the stories of how Canadian women have followed their dreams I will give you insight and inspire you.

Chapter One:
Beginning With the Plan

Dreams not pursued by action are simply that, dreams with little prospect of being attained.

Action taken without a plan or direction is simply that — action with little prospect of success.

Tie the plan and the action together and the dreams can become reality.

Julie V. Watson

No matter whether you are beginning a new business, revamping an existing one, or are successful and happy with what you are doing but want to keep on the right track for the future, there are a few steps that can help keep things progressing in your chosen direction.

- The first step is to define your goals — both for your business aspirations and your personal life. They cannot be separated.
- The second step is to create a plan.
- The third step is to do it.

I am not talking about the traditional business plan. I am advocating a life plan to take you to your goals, related to both earning an income and improving your personal life.

It is also important for women to recognize that we play by our own rules, often with different priorities than men. We tend to choose different types of businesses. That is not wrong, nor does it need defending — it just is.

Acceptance of the differences enables us to pursue our own goals in our own ways. Be wary of being directed to emulate how men do things because their methods are better or their success rate is higher. Use the act of planning to map your own path.

"The day-to-day experiences of women entrepreneurs differ from those of men due to very fact that they are women. Their life experiences are different from those of men, they often lack business experience, and they are socially conditioned differently from men. The concerns and responsibilities of women are different from those of men due to their respective roles in society, the family, and the business world."

Prime Minister's Task Force on Women Entrepreneurs Report and Recommendations, October 2003

I am going to use myself as an example of following the life plan aspect. In the early 1970s my husband, Jack, and I decided we wanted a change in our lives. We were in a situation in which many people find themselves. We were both working — me for a large manufacturer, he for the government. We had one son, who was typical of kids his age in the soon-to-be-mega-city of Brampton/Bramalea, Ontario, in that he divided his time between school, hockey, the mall, and hanging on the street with his friends. We were purchasing a typical subdivision home, acquiring the usual "stuff," and managed to go somewhere for a holiday once a year.

Trouble was, both Jack and I were dissatisfied with our lives. The sameness of every day. The lack of adventure. The stress put on us by family and jobs. The time spent commuting. The hustle, the bustle, the sheer number of people. The feeling of being a little cog on a big wheel that someone else was driving.

It all combined to set us on a path to find a better life. We looked west. In fact, at one point, we sold our furniture and tried to find work in British Columbia. Money ran out before jobs appeared so we waited a couple more years, working to acquire another start-up fund.

Between forays seeking "the perfect place," we took a vacation in Prince Edward Island. It was our third or fourth visit. As we rolled off the ferry at Borden, we all three gave out a big sigh.

"It feels like home," says I.

"What are we doing looking in places like Calgary and Vancouver when this is here?" replied Jack. We spent the vacation looking at this place with new eyes. Returning home we announced our decision to move to Prince Edward Island. Within a few months it was a done deed. Jack and John settled in to our new life quickly with job and school getting them out in the community, making new friends, finding a life. I had a harder time. I had to take a job that was a huge step down from my administrative assistant position for a large automotive manufacturer. It was the lack of employment at a level that I was used to that led me to becoming a freelance writer.

I had arrived in P.E.I. determined to get a job just until I was able to establish myself as a craftsperson, developing the pottery business a friend and I had played at on a part-time basis (in addition to our full-time jobs).

After searching for over a year, and constantly being told I was overqualified, I finally lied about my abilities and took a job as a receptionist. After a year of getting coffee and being called "dear" I needed change. No one actually patted me on the head, but I lived in constant dread that they were going to.

So, there I was, stuck in a dead-end, demoralizing job and needing to change for my own sanity. For the first and only time in my life I became depressed. I had gone from a vibrant corporate position and a life busy with friends and family to a boring, unfulfilling job and a lifestyle where my friends and family were absent and my interests not being fed.

It took the love and concern of my spouse and best friend to set me on the right path and change my future. I often tell the story of this phase of my life when giving workshops to businesswomen or writers on using five- or ten-year planning to change one's life and attain goals. It demonstrates several things:

- Firstly, that we benefit from the support of others. We should seek it when we need it, accept it when offered, and pass it along when we can.

- Secondly, we need a plan. We need it because if you don't know your destination, it is darn near impossible to make the right turns to get you there.
- Thirdly, we need to think beyond the boundaries of any plan. Look at developing your life path or business like a trip or voyage. You have many destinations along the way and are happy to reach them, to pause for a time and savour. But they don't mean the end of the journey; there are always new discoveries to be made, new adventures to be had.

So, back to my story. Things all came to a head one fall day when my friend Helen came over to the Island from her home in Pictou. She and Jack were having a grand time talking about the things they were doing, common interests in work — all manner of things. We had become friends with Helen and her husband, Roy, in Ontario. She and Jack worked together.

When they decided to move back home to Nova Scotia at about the same time we decided to move to P.E.I., it seemed like fate was sending a message. Helen and I had shared many happy hours making crafts, studying pottery, and attending craft fairs, and we had a vision of continuing to do so.

Unfortunately, that didn't happen. The necessity of holding down full-time jobs limited free time. Geographically we look close on a map — at least as the crow flies — but the reality was I had moved to an island. During the summer we could travel by ferry, a three-hour trip minimum door to door. Heavy traffic could mean that trip took five to eight hours. And then there was the cost. Even after Confederation Bridge was built across Northumberland Strait we were looking at three hours and at least one hundred dollars (toll and gas) per trip. There went the best-laid plans ...

We both quickly found that our pottery, candle making, and other crafts had been enjoyable because we so enjoyed the process when working together. Apart, neither of us had the heart for it. For a few years we managed some work on weekends, and had sessions each fall making pickles, jams, Christmas cakes, and candies, but gradually even that became more than we could manage in our busy lives.

Which brings us to the weekend that began a major change in my life. Listening to them chat, I suddenly felt overwhelmed with a sense of having no worth, no future. I left our farmhouse with our dogs, trudged down a hill through a potato field and into the woods. By now the tears were flowing freely. I remember throwing my arms around a tree and sobbing my heart out. To understand the importance of this event in my life you must know that I am normally one of the most optimistic, positive-thinking people. I almost never get depressed or experience that state of futility.

So, there I was hugging a tree, totally dejected. Just like the hero in a romance novel, Jack suddenly appeared, riding his horse, searching for me. After holding me while I blubbered all over him, he took me up behind him and back to the house. Told you it was romantic! There he and Helen took charge. I needed to get back some of the things I had enjoyed in the past. I needed to find purpose, they said.

A flyer had arrived that day listing night school courses. Helen and I had been night school junkies in Ontario, loving the combination of learning new things and meeting new people. It seemed a good place to start.

The choices were limited, but one caught our eye. It was a course of freelance writing. I had always enjoyed writing letters and such. There might be interesting people there. And it certainly sounded better than typing or bookkeeping or woodworking. Jack promptly wrote the cheque and signed me up.

I will never forget the first night of that class. The room was packed. There was a buzz of anticipation. These folks loved what they were doing. Writing, it seemed, was a passion with most of them. Our instructor was Hartwell Daley, a retired journalism instructor. Within the first ten minutes I realized that he was teaching marketing — the assumption being that every one of his students had written articles they wanted to sell. Little did he know that lurking three rows back from the front was an individual who had never put pen to paper with the idea of selling what she created. I was a grand letter writer, sending reams of paper across the Atlantic to cousins and friends left behind when we immigrated to Canada, but had never written anything even remotely resembling an article.

By the end of that first class I'd been bitten. I had the bug and desperately wanted to be part of this vibrant writing community. I also had a choice. Write something by next class or leave the course. I wrote something. Never did sell that first piece, a rambling tale of losing our passports and tickets the night before we were to fly home from London, England. But I did start something during that eight-week night school course that changed my whole life.

Hartwell put the focus on developing a writing career. To do that, he advocated, one must have a plan, a five- or ten-year plan.

"Look at it like a ladder," Hartwell said. "You need to break down the steps you need to take, and look at every one you achieve as a step up that ladder. Each step must be doable. Your goal is at the top."

So I got out my chart and started planning for a future of my choosing. Never before had I pictured in detail what lay in my future. Never had I thought in terms of actually itemizing where I wanted to go with life, or how I could get there.

It was the first time that I felt in charge. The process was euphoric.

Set doable goals that are achievable. Break them down into doable steps that will get you to that goal, decreed Hartwell. The key word was doable.

Where did I want to be in five years? What did I want to be doing? What things in my life would stand in my way? What was I willing to sacrifice? What was I *not* willing to sacrifice?

The first one was easy. I wanted to be earning my living from writing and I wanted to enjoy my work. I wanted to feel that I was benefiting from my work. What would stand in my way? My family. My reality was that my husband and son came first. I needed to have a steady income and I was not willing to compromise my family life in any way. They needed my financial input, but more important, my time and dedication to being the best wife and mother I could be. Jack had some medical problems that were a definite factor. We were, and are, a tight-knit family, and I would do nothing to endanger that in any way.

It took some work to develop a plan that would keep me on track. I needed to list steps that gave me a sense of making progress. So I began. The reality was that I could afford neither the time away from home nor the cost of going off to journalism school. That was *not* doable.

My first step was to continue taking courses from Hartwell. I vowed to attend every session he gave. And to do everything possible to further my knowledge in areas related to a writing career. Step one was to sign up for the next series of night courses. Step two was to write something good enough to market. Step three was to get published. And so it went. These *were* doable steps that I could fit into my family and work reality.

One week our assignment was to write a newspaper column with the subject of our choice. Since my husband had a horse and had become involved with the show horse circuit, that was a natural topic. It gave me an "in" into his world that did not require me to struggle into the saddle. I wrote a column about a horse show.

After reading it Hartwell told me to take it to the local newspaper, show it to the editor, and ask him if he was interested in it. I did and was told to leave it for the editor to look at. A week later I went to pick it up.

"Yes, dear," he said. "I liked what you wrote and I'm using it in tomorrow's paper."

"But," I sputtered, "you can't do that. I made it up. It isn't true." (This was, I thought, just a sample of what I *could* do if asked!)

"Well, dear [he always called me dear]," he said. "There's a phone over there, and a typewriter. You'd better go and write me a proper column that is true because the space is booked and you have to fill it."

I did. I felt so important sitting at that grubby desk in that grubby newsroom. I was a person transformed. "Saddletalk" was born and I was a columnist, supplying four to five hundred words every second week for the ripe sum of fifteen dollars. I was also class hero. I had a regular column in a newspaper. I had reached step three. With my pay I signed up for another session of Hartwell's course, which continued my pursuit of step one.

Now, since I could not stop working to go to college and study journalism, my step four was to find work that would act as my education. Say in a newspaper office.

While still taking classes every time Hartwell offered them I saw an ad in the newspaper, "Wanted Associate Women's Editor." Although my only related experience was a few weeks of writing "Saddletalk" and my only related education the sixteen evenings spent in Hartwell's night school courses, I applied for the job.

I was interviewed by the editor, who took me downstairs to the publisher's office. "Well, dear," they said. "You've written for us before. So you had better start as soon as you can."

I had reached step four.

I worked at the newspaper for five years. At the end of that time I had attained all of the goals I set down in my ten-year plan. While working days at the newspaper, I managed to sell some articles to magazines. I had also published my first book.

Following the method that Hartwell instilled in me I had broken down steps that I believed would help me get a book published. Step one, research the market to see what books are needed. Step two, write an outline for a book on that list. Step three, approach publishers to find one interested in my book. Step four, begin researching and writing the book, etc.

My research involved visiting every possible bookstore and shop that carried books and asking them what books they felt were missing from their shelves, what books they wanted to carry. I soon had a list of ten books. Number one was a seafood cookbook. Tourists, I was told, were always asking for that.

Author Julie Watson used "the plan" to attain her goal of becoming a recognized food writer. Here she is shown at a food show in Vancouver giving onstage cooking demonstrations — a lifestyle reward!

Seafood cookbook it was. Although my only expertise in the subject area lay with the fact that my mother had once worked in a fish and chip shop, I determined that I could write this book. With my market survey and outline in hand, I approached a local publisher, explained my idea, and got an immediate yes.

Building on the success of that first book, which sold steadily for fifteen years and is still asked for at craft fairs, I am now writing number seventeen, and have a contract in the works for my eighteenth book. Hundreds of my articles have appeared in publications in Canada and several other countries. More important than numbers, I have had the satisfaction of spending the last twenty years doing what I love to do. I take pride in my work. I also take pride in the fact that I sometimes compromised my own goals to accommodate the husband, son, parents, family, and friends I love so well. I purposely capped my ambition to keep a balance between my own goals and achievements and my family and personal life.

I have seen others pass me by and be showered with accolades, money, and a glamorous lifestyle. I have also seen those same people shed those who loved and cared about them. I have seen them hurt others in the climb for the top and ultimately hurt themselves. I'm proud of the fact that I always considered the impact of my decisions on other people before I acted on them. And of the fact that I willingly changed my direction without loading guilt on others or feeling sorry for myself.

In the long run, when I look back I feel I did good. I have two businesses, Creative Connections for writing/consulting and Seacroft to market my books.

I credit the plan, and the fact that I revised it periodically so that it always applied to my immediate future. I suggest that people never get far from their plan — physically far. I keep mine on the computer for easy revision and have a printout in a binder near my desk. The binder version also has pockets where I drop ideas I want to try, thoughts about future projects, things I don't want to forget.

Ask my friend Debbie, I live by binders. As great as the computer is, having a binder filled with sheet protectors is a wonderful aid for both planning and managing projects.

The Importance of the Plan

The success of my writing career compared to the failure of the pottery business is the perfect example of why we need to think through the steps we need to take to find success — the plan.

With the pottery we had not looked at the variables. We didn't take into account the distance, the expense of commuting, the marketing. I had thought I could sell from a home-based studio, but we had no tourism traffic past our home. I had also failed to take into account the very important fact that our pottery and craft business had worked in Ontario because we could spend hours working together while our spouses played hockey, watched hockey, took John to hockey, and did all kinds of "guy stuff." We didn't plan for Helen's three babies or my need to spend vacations going to see family left in Ontario.

We just plain didn't think it through.

When I moved into a writing career I had a plan that took into consideration my family commitments, my chosen lifestyle, where I wanted to go with my writing business, and feasible ways of getting there. It worked.

Now I'm again in the process of revamping what I do. Just a few days ago I celebrated the big six-oh. It is, without doubt, a milestone in life. Strangely, I feel more energetic, more enthusiastic about the future, and in better health that I have for years. That is partly because of the revamp.

I find the process of actively thinking through what I want to do, where I want to focus my energy, and what I will focus on to be as good as a shot of adrenaline.

So out comes my five-year plan. For me, at this time in life, five years is the smart number to focus on. For in five years I will have an income from my pensions, so then I will change my plan again.

Here are my realities and priorities for now.

I'm going to focus on what I enjoy and what will make me more money because we are in a cash crunch caused by my husband's medical problems, by family deaths (and the long illnesses that preceded them) that required a great deal of unanticipated travel and, for me as a freelancer, lost income, and by a two-year period of "if it can possibly break it will" expenses.

My career focus will be three pronged:

- First, I want to secure markets for my writing that are steady. Although I thrive living a little on the edge, we are finding the inconsistent cash flow hard now that Jack took an early retirement for health reasons. Having regular money is important.
- Second, I love writing books, and they provide ongoing income. I still receive royalty payments for books I wrote in the 1980s. Books I write now will become my pension fund if I choose the right

topics. That is important because like so many self-employed people I was not able to pay maximum payments into Canada Pension and so will receive a reduced benefit. Both of these things will be focused on the topics or areas of interest that I feel passionate about: entrepreneurship, self-help for women, travel and cuisine, and recording the fun and interesting things of our past that I enjoy.

- Third, I want to get into direct selling of my books and other products. Writing is a rather solitary occupation, so I love getting out to craft fairs and such. I also love going places. Since Jack took an early retirement he feels the need to supplement our income, even if he only earns the money to pay for golf, skating, lottery pools with his coffee buddies, and some extra travelling. His poor health and rapidly deteriorating eyesight limit his job possibilities, so we are going to focus on flea markets, craft fairs, and such.

At first glance this plan doesn't seem all that different from my plan of years ago. Proof that I have been focused on what I like to do and what works for me for several years now. Proof that, for me anyway, the planning works.

Things On My Current Ladder

- To accumulate enough money to invest so that I can have an income from it, allowing me to slow down just a tad
- To buy (and fully pay for) a motorhome before I slow down
- To continue to learn and to expand my knowledge in areas that give me pleasure
- To publish my own books
- To work more with my son, publishing works together
- To have a successful retail marketing operation centred around craft fairs and a mail-order business
- To get back to travelling
- To help Jack, my husband, establish his own niche at craft fairs and such

- To pay off the mortgage
- To spend time helping my aging parents and other family members and friends — to give back

My Realities

- Husband is tied to home ownership
- A retired husband is more expensive to maintain than a working one — I want him happy, occupied, and able to enjoy the things that he likes to do
- Jack's health is deteriorating
- Our retirement income is not what it should be
- It costs $2,000 (minimum) every time I visit John or the parents
- Arthritis — I hurt and have to work at maintaining my own health
- My energy levels are getting harder to maintain
- Aging parents, who are not particularly supportive of me and who are becoming increasingly dependent
- I'm falling behind new technology and need to upgrade my skills

The What-if Solution

Having trouble nailing down the details of your plan? Trouble thinking ahead two or three years, let alone five or ten? Try reverse thinking — asking yourself the "what-if" question.

What if I don't go for it and try my ideas? Will I regret it later on?
What if I can't get a bank loan? Can I prepare an alternate plan?
What if I put my plan ahead of family concerns? Will it affect my future relationships?
What if I talk it over with my spouse and we come to a compromise? Can I live with that?
What if I get a large order? Can I fill it? Do I want to go into large-scale production?

Running through the "what-ifs" can save you a lot of headaches down the road and provide innovative answers to many questions that had seemed impossible to answer. It also makes you realize that many things that we give huge importance to really don't matter all that much.

What if I don't get a new car? Well, I drive the old one, or take a cab.
What if I don't get that contract? I get off my duff and look for another.
What if I don't get funding or a loan? I seek other options, or downscale my plans to affordable steps
What if my product doesn't sell? I'll do market testing to see why, and look at other options. I'll also endeavour to recoup as much money as I can to invest in another project.

No matter what the scenario, there is a next step, a solution. The secret is to always have a backup, another path you can follow to the same destination.

I remember my grandfather used to say, "I might have to go fields way, but I'll get there." He was referring to the fact that he didn't have a car and might have to go on foot through the fields, but he would get there.

Mission Statement

There is a theory at work with all of my planning and filling in charts and forms. If you write it down, you are visualizing it and have a commitment to following through. Making a statement on paper encourages you to live up to it. Just the very act of thinking it through clarifies both the goal and how to achieve it.

Although the very thought of it increases the yawn factor tenfold, working to come up with a good mission statement can be very beneficial.

The act of doing it forces you or your company to focus on the business and its future direction and its goals. It helps you avoid costly errors and time-consuming distractions.

Mission statements should:

- be simple: a short statement of what business you are in, what you do;
- reflect who you are;
- reflect what you or your company does;
- reflect who you do it for; and
- list factors that allow you to achieve your goals: values, principles, and philosophies that articulate how the mission will be accomplished, day to day and into the future.

Once you have a good mission statement, use it. Share it with clients and potential customers by including it on your letterhead or in handout material. Make it visible to yourself and your employees, especially new employees.

Revisit and revise your mission statement regularly.

Business Plans

There are dozens of resources out there on doing the traditional business plan — and you will need one if you plan to seek funding or financing, or to simply direct your production and marketing. My advice is to go to various banks, government business service centres, or the library for advice. Quite often you need to write a specific plan to suit the bank, government department or agency, or organization you are presenting it to. So ask them for their guidelines.

Most of us dislike the process of doing business plans and neglect giving them the time they require. But with costs of everything escalating so rapidly, none of us can afford to "fly blind."

One thing I will stress about any plan, be it your personal growth plan or a formal business plan, is that it must be revisited from time to time. I try to review my plan every January, or when a major goal has been achieved. There are also many other triggers:

- If goals change, redo your plan.

- If things are not going well, if you feel you are struggling, redo your plan.
- When things are going well but you don't want to stagnate, redo your plan.
- When business grows and you don't want to stay static, redo your plan.
- When changes in owners, top management, location, or product lines happen, redo your plan.
- When there are changes in trends or the economy, redo your plan.

Identifying Good Business Ideas

Many, many times we hear the same questions: "Where do you get your ideas?" and "How do you know a good idea?" Truth is, most of us don't really know the answer to those questions. Good ideas just pop into our heads, or at least it seems that way. To facilitate this epiphany:

- Be observant about trends or patterns in consumer consumption. Entrepreneurs have a distinct advantage if they recognize trends, patterns, and changes before others and get to the market ahead of the competition.
- Don't overlook the obvious. There is nothing more upsetting than having someone come in and succeed at something that was right there in front of you. Take a good thoughtful look around.
- Pay attention to the small things. Many of the best opportunities lie with small items or services that are easily overlooked.
- Watch for products or services that are good ideas but are being poorly done. Can you improve on them and find an opportunity for yourself?
- This is the era of combined services. Bookstores and coffee shops, laundromats and bars. Are there things that you can combine for a unique business? Perhaps with a partner?
- Be an avid reader and researcher, seeking out information about new, general unknowns. Journals, trade magazines, and industry newsletters all help you keep on top of things and gather infor-

mation. Reading material in university libraries and government offices is often cutting-edge.

- Talk to everyone you can. What better way to find out needs and requirements than by talking? Trade shows, networking sessions, business meetings — talk the talk.
- Keep a receptive and open mind to allow new ideas in.

This book is a collection of shining examples of people with great ideas and the moxie to act on them. The amazing thing is that for every one I have included, there are tens — no, hundreds — of other more innovative concepts and great ideas.

On the following pages you will find questions and sample forms to help you start your own planning process. Easily duplicated on a scratch pad or by using tables on your computer, these detail the steps you should take to define both your destinations and your steps on the ladder when creating your five- or ten-year plan.

Setting long-terms goals of five or ten years may seem just too far away, but for many of us current life circumstances mean that we can't, or choose not to, pursue things we dream of right now. Take the case of a single mom. With kids to raise, a full-time job, limited finances, and responsibilities too numerous to mention, she probably can't follow her dream of backpacking around the world and writing a book based on her travels, at least right now. But she can be taking the steps needed to enable her to do those things later on. The reality is, in ten years her kids will be more self-sufficient and she will be able to ready herself for a goal that demands preparation. And just think of the fun, of the interesting life she can have in the meantime.

- She can get the education she needs through reading, taking short courses, attending workshops, and by simply doing.
- She can get experience backpacking by enjoying weekends out hiking and camping both with and without her kids.
- She can ensure that she is physically fit so that when she is ready she will be able.
- She can gain experience as a writer by writing about places she goes, local outdoor activities, and local travel destinations.

- She can get established as a freelance writer, especially in the highly competitive field of travel writing.
- She can learn everything she can about her anticipated destinations.
- She can learn the processes of journaling, of preparing a book outline, of doing research, of approaching publishers.
- She can pursue work in a field related to her goals, perhaps as a travel agent or at a newspaper.
- She can join groups or organizations that are associated with her goals and take advantage of things that they provide.
- She can start a savings account. Even a couple of dollars a week will provide a nice nest egg for her trip.
- She can go public with her plan, enlisting support from those around her. Or, she can keep it private, hold it close to savour and to sustain her until it reaches the close to reality stage.

The list of things you can be doing toward a goal is endless.

If these things are written down, you are aware that you are progressing, that steps are being taken toward your goal. This is a very important element of planning. When you can see progress being made toward *your* goals enthusiasm remains high, you keep on track. Your attitude remains positive and you begin approaching life as an achiever, not just a dreamer.

Those end goals may change. By the time our gal is ready for her around-the-world trip she may realize that backpacking and sleeping in a pup tent no longer have the appeal they once did. So, the plan is revised to include accommodation and less physically demanding transportation than her own two feet.

Using the Plans

- Draw up forms that work for you and make a few copies so that you feel comfortable revising them.
- This is a process that should take a little time. Much of what I suggest you define takes time to think about and mull over.
- In my classes I suggest everyone go with their gut reaction and

answer on the spot as part of our exercise. Then I ask them to think about their personal life and how those things will impact on it.

- Think carefully about what you are willing to sacrifice for your goals, where compromise might be best for all, and look for the solution that provides balance between your dreams and your realities.

- Break things down into truly doable steps. Don't just say "get training" or "pursue a degree." Break that down. List your options: can you get that training in a slower, but less invasive, way, perhaps as a part-time student? Are there workshops nearby, or should you seek out sessions away from home and spend part of your vacation attending them?

Make a point of seeking out professional or special interest organizations that will help you attain your goals. Make getting involved a goal. Make attending their conferences a goal.

Plans should be revisited and revised at least once a year. Try taking a quiet time around the New Year to get out your plan, note steps made up your ladder toward your goal, revise any goals or steps, or simply get yourself back on track. This is a much better way of welcoming the New Year than making silly resolutions that you won't keep. These resolutions are real; they are a lifestyle.

I like to keep my old plans so that I can look back and see the progress I've made. What a great way to pat myself on the back or reaffirm my sense of achievement and self-worth. That's why I maintain a planning binder. It not only records where I've been, but also where I'm going, and reminds me that with proper dedication to the plan I can reach the goals I set for myself.

Joanne Zinter turned a love of making condiments into a very successful home-based business. Beginning with favourite home recipes for antipasto and jalapeno jelly, and quickly adding orange brandied cranberries, she began selling at the Edmonton farmers' market. Many flavours and fusions were on the burner: peachy mango chutney, award-winning roasted garlic and onion jam, and roasted garlic pepper pot.

In order to make large amounts that could be bottled and sold retail, Joanne tested the recipes in her own kitchen, working up to a commercial batch of twelve hundred small jars, with the help of a government-run food processing development centre. Today she makes fifteen different products (and is constantly developing for the future), fills sixty thousand jars a year, and is distributed throughout North America. She sells retail and through mail order and has also developed a second label for wholesaling to the grocery store market.

Joanne followed our suggested method of slow development and offers some advice for others:

- Definitely see what assistance the government offers and use it to your advantage.
- Don't go fast. Take the time to plan your development.
- Be prepared for hard work: "If I had any inkling how much work it would be I don't think I ever would have done it, working full-time, making products on weekends, selling at markets, going to gift shows — for ten years I went full out. Six years ago I quit nursing, so in those six years business has really grown because I've devoted the time to it. And when I quit work I went to Italy for four months to a cooking school — a neat experience."
- Slow development meant that she was able to finance herself, other than a small start-up loan from her father, which she paid back in six months.
- Don't quit your day job until you get established. "When I first started and was working full-time there was no way this business could have made me a living. There are so many costs at first, you don't have volume, you just have to establish market base before leaping in. You can also write losses off against your income — that helps too."
- Take advantage of opportunities for promotion through interviews, trade shows, and so on.

For more about Joanne Zinter, refer to chapter 2, "Pursuing your Passions."

Use the following forms, questions, and suggestions as a guideline for developing your own business and personal plans.

Name: _____

Date: _____ **Place:** _____

Where I Am Today (Brief Description of Your Life): _____
_____
_____
_____
_____
_____

If I Could Have, or Be, Anything I Want, My Wish Would Be: _____
_____
_____
_____
_____

My Life Plan

Before you can plan your future business, you need to know where you are in your own life. Answering the following will help you to focus.

1.   If I could be or do anything I want in the whole world, what would it be?

2.   What is my personal reality?

3.   What is my realistic dream?

4.   What do I love to do for me?

5. What things do my family love to do?

6. How can I bring together what I love and need with my life realities and family needs?

7. What is most important to me?

8. What gives my life meaning?

9. What do I want to be and do in my life?

10. When I'm seventy and retiring, what do I want people to say about me?

11. When I look back at my life, what will I regret if I don't do it?

Skills Inventory

Another important thing everyone needs to do is realistically assess your skills. Do an inventory of what you can do, what you are good at, and put it on paper.

Don't be shy. List all of the things you can do. List everything that you are good at. Great with people? Good with numbers? Great organizer? Good woodworker? List them all.

Things I Want to Accomplish With My Career:	Things I Want to Accomplish With My Family or Personal Life:

My Plan: _____ Date: _____	
Steps That Will Take Me Up My Entrepreneurial Ladder:	**Steps That Will Take Me Up My Personal Ladder:**

Chapter Two:
Pursuing Our Passions

If it doesn't matter to you more than the potential for making money, it's going to be difficult to make a success of it.
Marianne Bertrand, Muttluks Inc.,
winner of the Innovation Award,
Rotman Canadian Woman Entrepreneur
of the Year Awards

I won't ever claim to be an expert but ... my advice is, if you have a good idea that you believe in, go for it. If your motivation is money only, you may not make it. You have to really enjoy what you do and let the success come.
Jackie Kevill, Loony Lizard Dollar Stores,
winner of the Impact on Local Economy Award,
Rotman Canadian Woman Entrepreneur
of the Year Awards

I have a theory that success comes most easily — and more important, most enjoyably — when you follow your passions. The fact that you love what you do is better than all the money in the world. The financial rewards are a bonus.

In the course of my work I meet hundreds of women achievers who have that special spark. Some have big businesses; others have businesses so small they are barely recognized. These women in business (WIBs) range from owning a film production company to writing romance novels, from building microwave ovens for thawing plasma to designing furniture that symbolizes the Haida culture, from photographing flower mosaics to creating little people from natural findings, from offering doggie adventure vacations to hand-making tiny tack for model horses.

The tie that binds them is that they love what they do. They also tend to be fiercely independent, wanting to do things in their own way.

The key to this kind of business success is, it seems, taking an interest in something that is enjoyed and incorporating it into your life by creating work related to it. Sounds complicated? It isn't. Many women have turned something they are passionate about into their life's work.

Take golf. Long thought of as a man's game — at least by men — golf is providing wonderful opportunities for women. And they are tremendously varied, as you will see. As you read through our sampling of women working in golf, keep two things in mind. First, these women are all working in a small area of the country, my home province of Prince Edward Island. Imagine the opportunities if you think on a national scale! We haven't touched on dozens of potential golf-related opportunities.

Secondly, we are using golf as one example. You can find as much variety and opportunity in other interest areas — just use your imagination and your smarts to find your niche. As you read on you will also realize that some of these women are not what is typically thought of as an entrepreneur. First, we have a pro golfer. Not a business, you think. Well, think again. Any career that is based on yourself and your skills in the manner of professional sports is indeed a business. One of the keys to success is that those who are successful treat what they do as a business. They may not give it that label, but that is what they do. They, or people who work for/with them, manage what they do — their cash flow, their bookings, their scheduling. They may hire help, but they are in control.

Golfer With Moxie: Lori Kane

Lori Kane, a local gal playing on the LPGA circuit, has been one of my idols for a long time. Not because she is number one. She isn't. Even so, she has done rather well on the professional golf circuit, earning herself a nice income while living a life she truly enjoys. For Lori to attain the level she has she had to have the passion for the game, the tenacity and courage to leave the comfort of home and go for it, and the moxie to stay the course. While Prince Edward Island has more than its fair share of golf courses, it is certainly not in the mainstream when it comes to competitive golf, especially professional-level tournaments for women. So here is Lori, playing a sport she loves, travelling the world, earning a better income than she could ever hope for here in Canada's smallest province, and receiving accolades from far and near for her sense of fair play and sportsmanship along with playing a darn good round of golf. Lori crossed the $4-million mark in career earnings in 2002, a year when she lost in a one-hole, sudden-death playoff to Annika Sorenstam, one of two second placings behind golf's superstar. At the date of writing, she had placed in the top ten in eleven of twenty-seven starts in 2003 and had four career victories to her credit. Pretty good life I say, whether she ever makes number one or not!

A Lifelong Golfing Affair — Her Way: Anne Chouinard

Anne Chouinard has come a long way since the days when her golf pro dad carried her around on his golf bag, progressing from using cut-down clubs to "play" the family backyard in Quebec, which she laughs "seemed awfully long," to a career as director of golf at the Canadian Golf Academy in Prince Edward Island.

That early exposure set her on a path to recognition as a top-notch golf instructor with a no-nonsense approach. Among those benefitting from her expertise is Lori Kane, who ranks as the country's top female golfer. Ann, Lori's swing coach, flies to work with her when needed.

Although there was a time when the game didn't seem "fast enough" for the athletic young woman, she played as an amateur while attending Laval University. Degree in psychology in hand, she decided to give professional golf a try before hanging up her clubs.

"I turned pro in '88, went south and joined the Futures Tour, one notch under the LPGA." In 1989, Anne became the first woman in sixty-eight years to qualify to play the Quebec PGA Men's Tour.

"When I became a member of the CPGA in Quebec, we were eight or nine women in the program. Basically I was the first woman to try and to qualify for the Men's Tour so I played the whole tour with the men. It was a good experience."

She spent ten years as a golf pro, becoming Head Professional in 1994. Accomplishments as a player include du Maurier Series and Central Florida Challenge Tour wins. In the final stage of qualifying for the LPGA, reality hit.

"I thought, wow!, what if I qualify? I felt something might be missing. I didn't feel that I was going to fulfill myself totally by playing," she said, laughing. "I felt guilty playing for a living."

Instead she opted to "help people enjoy the game, have more fun, help get kids started." It had always been in her mind. While playing the pro tour she completed a five-year CPGA apprenticeship, including operation of a golf course and teaching. In 1994 and 1995, Anne travelled south with Lori Kane to play golf. Recognition of each other's talents led her to coaching Kane, and to Prince Edward Island.

"The owners were looking for someone to head the Academy programs. She gave them my name. One thing that really appealed was starting something new, with a team of pros, to work together and exchange ideas. The concept of starting and building — it was a vision I've had for years. We work, we learn, as a group. That's why I said yes. It was a dream come true."

As well as working with adults, Anne instills youngsters with her love of golf through junior camps, saying the benefits are legion. "It's not only about golf with kids. It's more about good values of life; we teach teamwork, respect for each other. We don't laugh at the little kid who can't do it. We teach etiquette. Golf is a great game for that. Consideration of others is passed along right up through competition."

She adds, "There aren't many places where parents can go out with kids and do something fun together." And, she says, there are few environments where parents can read their kids. "If you pay attention you can see if they get down on themselves, or keep morale up — parents can learn a lot out there on the course."

With golf and family as focal points of her life, she has the satisfaction of seeing her early visions materializing

"I love the variety, the challenge. There are so many things; contact with people, the opportunity to help them. Most people who come here are a little desperate with golf. Being given opportunity to see a student going 'Wow.' Seeing them believe that they can do it. That is my biggest 'high.'"

It is experience that stands Anne Chouinard in good stead in a field that many perceive as male-dominated.

"In the industry a good number of women are teaching, pros, members of the CPGA. There are probably 250 women as pros in the country who are teaching at different clubs. Men appreciate what we can do. Most of them see us as their equal."

She says the key is how you approach it. "If you are competent, professional and have integrity things will go well for you. It's a matter of your perception. Of course if you go in thinking you are inferior ..."

Setting the Course — Golf Course That Is: Merina Currie

Another area where women excel in golf is as course owners and operators. Any given day from May through October will find Merina Currie looking after management of the pro shop, staff, advertising, supplies, and accounting of Glen Afton Golf Course in Prince Edward Island while her husband handles superintending, the grounds, "and etc." Merina has tackled most jobs involved with providing a course for one of the fastest growing sports in the world. For her complete story, and her advice for other WIBs, see chapter 8, "It's a Family Affair."

Island Tee Times Reaps Awards: Amanda Stewart and Maureen Kerr

A golf ball sitting atop a tee waiting for a golfer to swing the club and connect is the perfect logo for Island Tee Times, the business that garnered a Young Entrepreneur Award for Prince Edward Islanders Amanda Stewart and Maureen Kerr.

Not bad for two young students who came up with the concept as a school assignment. And they are, in the words of the president of Business Development Bank, "emblematic of a phenomenon where people creating their own jobs end up creating new business-es and ultimately new work for others." In my words, they did it right, starting in a way that was financially viable and growing at a steady rate.

"We are a golf packager," they say when asked to describe their business. "We do golf packages to bring people from away to Prince Edward Island. We can set up as much or as little as they want. Flights, accommodation, tee times, or just tee times if that's all they require."

Grins Maureen, "We're able to take care of the whole holiday for people — the takeoff and landing, the beer waiting in the fridge, a rental car and a map with directions. They love us."

The majority of their business involves setting up the whole vacation. "People like one-stop shopping," says Amanda. "They pay one price. Two weeks before arrival they pay us, then everything is all paid. They don't have to take out their wallet every time they do something."

They estimate that 80 percent of their business comes from men, who "appreciate it the most. Women are shoppers. Women will check around. As soon as a man finds a place that will do everything they stop, and they're not leaving."

Their clientele is usually upper scale, and includes a lot of business-men, usually travelling in fours. They also get a lot of "school buddies" getting together. Most are between the ages of thirty and fifty and are "quite avid" golfers.

The business is growing at an awe-inspiring rate. Island Tee Times booked golf games for thirty customers in 1999. In 2003, the company arranged golf packages for six hundred clients. Recently they formed a partnership with Golf PEI, the marketing association for the golf industry in the province, to open the first reservations centre offering a toll-free service for North American golfers to reserve tee times on twenty-five Island courses. It will be an extension of their one-call-does-all service.

As well, the dynamic duo is starting to work with the industry in New Brunswick, and they have their eyes set on Nova Scotia and parts of Ontario.

So how did these two twenty-somethings come so far, so fast? They were both students at the Atlantic Tourism and Hospitality Institute in 1999.

"Maureen started when we were in school," explains Amanda. "She was pregnant and working at a restaurant but knew she couldn't be on her feet much longer. She also wanted to be at home with her son, so decided to go into business."

In school they had a class called entrepreneurship and had to conceptualize a business.

"Maureen did hers on this and mine was similar, involving organizing family vacations to P.E.I. When we were done, Maureen said 'Okay, I'm going to do it.' She took the same business plan, and did it."

They formed a partnership in 2000. Working from home, Maureen began by offering a golf booking service. When Amanda joined the firm she had purchased a travel franchise that allowed their company to book flights, accommodations, and automobile rentals.

In 2003 they left Maureen's home and moved into a new office space. They also hired a third person to work with them, and will be expanding even more with the new reservation service.

"We owe our success to the fact that we provide value-added service and work hard for each and every one of our clients. It is also important to maintain a positive outlook while you are growing a business, and we have continued to do that."

While they don't feel that there was any opposition to them because they were two young women, they did have to work to be taken seriously.

"It's interesting. We did a big presentation for a huge contract and were the only women in the room presenting to all men — mostly older men. It's a mind block, but we haven't let it get us down. I don't think they took us seriously for the first couple of years, but now know we are a voice to be reckoned with. We are certainly not in the old boys' club, they don't always think to include us in what is going on."

Island Tee Times does the majority of its promotion on the internet through their web site, which has been top-rated by search engines. They also take advantage of links and are on the government's tourism web site and the PEI Vacation Guide. Hiring someone to do their web site is a small portion of their budget, but well spent.

Amanda Stewart and Maureen Kerr credit their business success to being able to provide custom-tailored holidays, even as their client list mushrooms. They say:

- Know your business. In their case, they said what they sell is knowledge. Someone booking a vacation doesn't know the region, what hotels are near the courses, what the different courses offer. "We see pretty well everything that we book. So when people call and say what is in this cottage, what condition is it in, we know. Similar thing with golf courses. We know where they are, what they look like, who is there."
- Learn from others in your business. In their case they studied other golf booking services, and they also feel they benefitted from their school, where both tourism and golf are on the curriculum. "We had all the resources there in school and so many people in the industry to draw on."

Cashing In On the Links ... Or Breaking Those Grass Ceilings

As important as its role is in providing business opportunities for women entrepreneurs, golf is also described as a "hot" business driver. For decades men have been using time on the course to cement relationships with clients and as a perk to lure decision-makers to look upon their company with favour.

It is an equalizer, a networking opportunity that has few equals. Yet women have not been taking advantage of it. The question is, why? According to the experts, the answer is fear. The solution is to tackle the challenge, learning enough to get over the fear and enjoy.

Golf can be intimidating for the first-timer, but if women learn to utilize this powerful business tool, they'll be one more step up the ladder, and they will benefit from the fresh air and exercise as well.

The golf course holds a special appeal, one that non-golfers can't always appreciate. It's hard to understand the pleasure found in whacking a small white ball around a great big groomed lawn then chasing it down in a motorized cart that resembles those bumper cars at the midway. It's harder still to "get" the concept of why golf works.

A little research reveals that the game has broad appeal because it puts everyone on an even footing, in a relaxed environment. At least that's what they say. Anyone who knows my spouse knows that the desire to beat previous scores, beat par, putt better, and be the best does bring its own level of stress!

But from a business point of view, a game of golf eliminates organizational rank, helps develop contacts, puts things on a less formal basis, and often generates contacts and leads that are a big plus later on.

To get the scoop, we contacted Ann Worth, executive director of the Atlantic Canada Food Export Partnership. Ann, a believer in the benefits of networking on the golf course, is known for the golfing events she's put together.

"I think it's invaluable. A great relationship builder. Look at the volume of corporate golf tournaments," she says. "I almost developed a business around corporate golf."

Involvement with trade associations took her away from that concept, but Worth still considers the game an important "tool." Among those on the golf course, she says, there are two types of serious golfers (aside from recreational or fun players). "It's a great opportunity. Basically there are two types of golfers. Those that really work it for networking all the time, and those who are serious about their score and don't want even a whisper while they play." Problems, she chuckles, can arise when those types are mixed, so be careful how you put together a foursome.

"Then there are people like me who just want to have a good time."

She adds, "They say you can tell a lot about a person, about how they conduct themselves, their integrity, how they handle things — insight into their makeup. You see how people perform under pressure. If you are going to be doing business with them its good to have that insight about the person you are going to deal with."

Benefits continue off the course. Once you've shared a game or two you are in the loop, have something in common to talk about that is not related to business, and as a result are often seen as more credible, with a competitive advantage. And don't forget shared time and experiences can result in leads that just might prove valuable.

It all comes down to building relationships, creating shared moments, and spending quality time with prospects while you gain insight into their personality and conduct.

Oh, and having fun. As a new golfer I can attest to the fact that the ability to laugh at oneself — and a rule that no score can go above double par — can make for a grand few hours. Just remember than golf is a dignified sport, where consideration for others rules!

Golf Networking Tips
- Do know the rules
- Do practice good etiquette — be polite
- Do be prepared — lessons might be a good idea
- Don't talk business
- Don't take your cell phone!
- Don't tell the other guy how to swing, hit, putt, or anything
- Don't smoke or drink alcohol
- Don't cheat

Jobs With Dogs

Another special interest area that is proving especially interesting to women is dogs. Canine cuties inspire passion — so much so that many women don't want to be parted from their furry friends, so they build a business that keeps the contact close. I first became aware of the close relationship between women and the canine friends through the television program *Dogs with Jobs* and decided I had to write a section called "Jobs with Dogs."

Muttluks Trendy Canine Footwear: Marianne Bertrand

I first read about Marianne Bertrand in a *National Post* supplement pro-filing the Rotman Canadian Woman Entrepreneur of the Year Awards for 2002. I stopped at her page because of an adorable picture of her with her basset hounds. So I went searching on the internet, found her web site, and learned what led to her Innovation Award for her business, Muttluks Inc., a fascinating WIB story.

Inspired by a gift of ineffective dog boots for her basset hounds, Marianne set out to build a better mousetrap, or in her case, a better dog boot. Thus was sown the seed of innovation, and Muttluks was born.

Encouragement for the concept came quickly when the first 130 sets sold out in less than a week to local Toronto-area pet stores that also recognized the need for quality canine paw wear. Marianne's entrepreneurial instincts had again proven right on the mark.

Before starting Muttluks, she had applied a similar "necessity is the mother of invention" logic to the construction business. Active as a consultant and designer in home renovations, her expertise in the environmental and non-toxic construction field developed out of health issues in her own life and her experience with environmental sensitivities. She recognized the opportunity to provide household audits and environmental renovations for people with allergies and sensitivities to building materials.

From a business standpoint, as she would later do with Muttluks, Marianne Bertrand had found a niche not being addressed in the marketplace. As a result of her innovations, the residential renovation company was awarded the Canada Mortgage and Housing Corporation (CMHC) 1995 Healthy Housing Award.

Marianne has also become a much sought after speaker. Her unique blend of entrepreneurial chutzpah and innovative product design is not only a winning combination, but has proven to be inspirational to novice entrepreneurs.

In fact, she could easily be taken for a Renaissance woman. Montreal born and raised, she holds a B.A. in Business Administration from Acadia University with a major in Accounting and Small Business. She is a graduate of the Canadian Securities Commission Course and also pursued a degree in Interior Design at Ryerson Polytechnic University. With new Muttluks products on the drawing board and her keen sense for developing innovative concepts, Marianne Bertrand personifies the entrepreneurial spirit of small business owners today.

"Follow your heart," says Marianne Bertrand, president of Muttluks Inc., after receiving her Rotman Canadian Woman Entrepreneur of the Year Award. "Of course your idea should make business sense, but it has to be more personally compelling than that. If it doesn't matter to you more than the potential for making money, it's going to be difficult to make a success of it."

Dogged Adventures: Kathryn Howell

When Kathryn Howell heard what a great time her husband had taking their pup on canoe trips, her "great idea light" went on and Dog Paddling Adventures was born. "The mission of our company is to bring people together who share a mutual interest in the wilderness and their pets," she says. "Our paddling, hiking and winter adventures allow for any dog lover to enjoy the outdoors (whether a beginner or experienced), while at the same time enjoying a bonding experience that is truly unique."

Today the Howells not only invite their clients to share the beauty of Ontario's finest lakes, rivers, and provincial parks with their furry friend on a Dog Paddling Adventure, they also offer skijoring and kick sledding in winter and hiking clubs in the spring and fall. As well, they produce the *Dog Paddling Post*, a newsletter with all kinds of doggy news, which is available on their web site. All Dog Paddling Adventures include camping accommodation, delicious meals, equipment, park permits, lifejackets and backpacks for both people and dogs, and the services of a wilderness guide.

For the story behind this unique business for the "doggy set," refer to chapter 8, "It's a Family Affair."

Worthy of Note

- A dog groomer, unhappy with working condition handling practices at a pet store where she was empl~~o~~y~~ ~~, set up her own service. With no facility for clients to visit, she now does a pet pickup and delivery — much to the delight of busy clients who happily pay a little extra for the convenience of having Fido returned home all spiffy and clean.

- Margaret L. Sawyer of Windy Hollow Stoneware in Edgetts Landing, New Brunswick, sells cat and dog headstones, as well as plaques and urns, making it possible for pet owners to lay their pets to rest in style. Every urn is hand finished to ensure the very best in quality.

- Jane Wentzell, owner of Invisible Fencing in Chester Basin, Nova Scotia, takes along Gideon, her border collie, when making calls. She believes his presence inspires confidence in customers because they recognize that as a dog owner she cares about her pet and wants what is best for them both, reported Gillian Thorpe in *Atlantic Progress*, May 1998.

- Elizabeth Lemire breeds, trains, and boards dogs at Chenil Cossak near St. Philippe, Quebec. *Home Business Report* magazine tells how word of mouth now brings all the business she can handle to this woman who looked at the trends and realized that the demand for smaller pets facilitated adding West Highland terriers to her breeding program, along with German shepherds. Developing a successful breeding business is a long-term venture made possible by offering obedience training. A smart move, as those who buy puppies continue their relationship, first through training, then through boarding.

- A huge growth area related to dogs involves pampering pet services. Dog walkers now have a professional association. Doggie daycares are popping up all over. One enterprising woman even has a service where she provides organic, gourmet meals especially selected for specific pets — and delivers the frozen entrees.

And then there are the thousands of opportunities for women in the food industry.

Tasty Treats: Joanne Zinter

Today's consumer has a limited amount of leisure time and as a result wants to minimize the time spent in the kitchen preparing food. With this in mind, Zinter Brown Taste Treats Inc. has created a line of gourmet "Taste Treats." All are delicious, attractive, easy to serve, and, for the adventurous cook, double as a taste infusion to create special recipes.

Photo courtesy of John Watson.

Edmonton's Joanne Zinter developed Zinter Brown Taste Treats Inc. into a gourmet delight of home-based success.

The business venture began in 1986 as a hobby, explains Joanne Zinter, who says she always liked to cook. A nurse by profession, she and a friend started to make antipasto to take to the market. They were always sold out by noon, a fact that inspired her to move ahead and develop other products. Off work on sick leave for a year and a half, she took advantage of the "development time."

A visit to Alberta Agriculture directed her to Leduc, Alberta, where she worked with food scientists. "They teach how to scale up recipes, do tests before starting any major production of products which makes sure they are stable, test shelf life, all of that kind of stuff," she said. "They helped me scale up the antipasto recipe, started with that first."

As well, she had to figure out all of the other aspects of food processing, label development (and the regulations around that), label design, and marketing.

"We started to market labelled product at the market and slowly got into some of the gourmet food stores in town — upper-class places — not grocery but basically gourmet food stores. The market was a fantastic place for taste testing. At that time you did not have to have an approved kitchen so we could do a product at home, taste test with the public at the market, get their response. Then, if it looked like being pretty popular, we would go out to Leduc and have them go through the same process.

"At that time, the government was just helping new companies with development of recipes and the first run. After that you were on your own and had to go out and find places to make product. I worked with Meals on Wheels, so rented that facility for a number of years, working on Saturday or Sunday because they were closed." They filled jars by hand, labelled by hand, and stored the product in the basement of the house. "You know what that means — up and down stairs!"

At the same time she was working full-time as a home care nurse.

"Did that for ten years, working full-time, making product, going to market, going to gift shows." As well, they attended craft shows, where retail sales became a big part of her income, along with wholesaling to stores. Trade shows have been added to her mix of sales activities. Joanne studies those shows, which are where she, as a wholesaler, seeks retailers to market her products.

"August shows are best," she shares, "this product sells best in the fall." Although nothing is predictable. In some instances she does two shows in one city, such as Edmonton.

"Along the way, I developed recipe brochures, did demos at the market where people would taste my product, also at stores I sell at. That's another way of marketing." She also developed a second label, selling her products as Zinter Brown on one label and Wedgewood Estate on the other. The two lines have different presentation to suit different markets.

"We put Wedgewood into a round 250 mL jar more for a grocery market, so that it wouldn't interfere with the more high end, Zinter Brown."

The higher end product is her main focus, because "margins go way down" when dealing with high volume. She says a margin of 30 to 40 percent is good in the food business. When dealing with big sales to supermarkets the norm is 10 percent or less.

Zinter Brown has won several awards for her products, including Best New Product for her Roasted Garlic and Onion Jam at the Fine Food Show in Toronto.

Joanne Zinter advises others to keep control of things like costs.

"It's all overhead if you have to build a plant, have to keep that plant going." After Meals on Wheels changed their policy about renting out their kitchens she had to look for other options and found her solution with the government facility.

"They now allow people to rent space at the plant at the Alberta Food Research and Development Centre in LeDuc so I just rent on daily basis. There is a pool of staff orientated to the plant. I call and line them up. We need about seven people, the area with the equipment, lots of freezer space and refrigeration."

She says this method of production "makes sense for sure. What I do is hire staff, book a day, arrange for ingredients to be delivered, also glass from Richards, labels from Winnipeg. Usually in a day we can do 200 dozen jars using their two 100-gallon kettles. They have an automated system for filling jars — the machine even puts lids on, then they come down to where we have tables set up to ensure jars are clean, and then label."

She also belongs to the Alberta Food Processors Association. "You have to have something new. If you do they will pay 50 percent of the cost for developing, going to shows in Canada and they helped with new labelling for one new product. It's a bit of a motivation to develop new products," she says, "very important in the end result. I have to pay a fee to belong, but I make up for that and more with rebates. If you're wanting to market, it's a great aid for marketing. Gets products out there."

Developing a recipe brochure has been an important step for the business. "It's really important; because you know, you go somewhere yourself and buy products, bring them home and put them in a cupboard. You never open them because you don't know what to do with it." That does not lead to second sales.

Joanne is a home-based business. "I do office work, phoning and etc. right out of the house. It helps when you don't have the overhead of an office and can write off some of the house expenses."

But she says being home-based is more than just a cost factor. There is the pleasure of being in your own space as well as the flexibility.

"It's so nice not to have to go to a job 8–4 every day. Sometimes I might work 14 hours in a day, but then I can always take time off to go away. I don't have to worry about holiday time, that sort of thing."

In the Spotlight

Getting up in front of an audience can turn knees into jelly and voices into quavering shadows of their former selves, and it can send our thought processes whirling away into outer space. Getting past the fear of being in front of an audience can open up new opportunities and, even better, bring about recognition of our accomplishments and successes. Whether making presentations, speaking, or showcasing your expertise at a conference, this is one of the best ways to market yourself and your business.

Not only is it personally rewarding, it can bring dollars into the coffers and get perks like paid expenses to events far from home. Becoming proficient as a speaker is something that can be accomplished by using our method of planning toward success. Small steps, planned to take you to your goal. Some examples of what you can do:

- Join volunteer groups that allow you to start practising in small group situations; they also open doors to attend conferences, give presentations, and speak.
- Connect with your audience by talking to them, not lecturing at them from behind a podium.
- Arrange to work with a microphone in advance of any presentation. The new clip-on mikes are much less intimidating than those big metal ones stuck in front of your face. If you are forced to use a standing microphone, arrive early so that you can test where it has to be and practise any adjustments. As a short person I've been in many situations where I had to stretch my neck like a crane because the microphone was too high.
- Work with your voice. Practice projecting authority and credibility by using a strong voice that doesn't lift at the end of sentences. The "lift" turns a statement into a question and makes you seem unsure of yourself.
- Be sure to practise your presentation or speech by reading it out loud several times. If it doesn't flow easily off the tongue, fix it well in advance.

> • Wear tried, true, and comfortable clothes and shoes with jewellery that complements but doesn't pull focus from what you are saying. If you have a new outfit or shoes, wear them ahead of time so that you know you won't get caught tugging a jacket closed, be distracted by pinched toes, or just not feel your best.

Passionate Dealer Parlays Innovation into Bargains: Jody Steinhauer

Jody Steinhauer has one personality trait that almost every one of us would envy — she loves to deal. This award-winning Toronto entrepreneur found her niche, capitalized on that talent, and formed the award-winning The Bargains Group Ltd.

When Jodi shares her vision and business advice, her message has the ring of validity that comes with knowing that what she says is based on personal experience.

With the dining room table as her office, the founder and president of The Bargains Group started out with a cell phone, a fax machine, a pager, and a pad of paper. She set out with innovation, skill, and tenacity to build her business. From a cash investment of $1,000, The Bargains Group has grown to a multi-million-dollar business that garnered her recognition as one of the best and brightest achievers in Canada through Canada's Top 40 under 40 Awards Program and the Rotman Canadian Woman Entrepreneur of the Year Award, Innovation Category!

Initially, her vision was to fulfill her dream in the clothing industry: to supply quality merchandise at the lowest prices to customers who wanted to build long-term relationships. Based on supply and demand, The Bargains Group Ltd. procures clearance wholesale clothing for customers across Canada. Relying on a complex and extensive network of suppliers and contacts, it is rare that Jody cannot find the product and meet the needs of her clients. Many times, she steps out of the box and procures items for people that are not included in her standard product mix. Jody has built her business successfully, growing from a one-woman operation to employing ten full-time staff in just twelve years, at the same time successfully balancing marriage and motherhood. She says her strong team, loyal customer base, and trustworthy suppliers have all contributed to her success. In fact, she says she doesn't believe in titles. Someone once referred to her as the CEO. It should have been, she says, CVO — chief visionary officer.

If entrepreneurs build their success on making the most of every opportunity, Jody truly embodies the entrepreneurial spirit. She is an example of how building long-term relationships, applying innovative marketing strategies, and taking risks, intent on results, can produce a stable and profitable business.

As she speaks to groups of businesswomen, Jody Steinhauer drops advice and tips for finding success at a rapid rate:

- It's okay to ask for help — to say "can you help me?"
- I strongly recommend any networking or sharing.
- There are no bad experiences, only opportunities. You just have to look at it in a different light.
- Service industries must rely on themselves and their reputation. Once you do something, and do a really good job, ask for a testimonial.
- Think of something that says you are different. You want them to go WOW! Really!
- When you go to people to network, keep it low-key.
- It takes a lot of work to get awards, but it is worth it. Gives you credibility!
- Work on the Hero Factor — if you are not their hero, they'll get another! You must be a hero in clients' transactions; even if you make a million deals successfully the one they will remember is the one that goes wrong.

Oceanographer Extraordinaire: Judith Bobbitt

Judith Bobbitt is a physical oceanographer who operates an environmental research and service company for the offshore industries. Already you can tell she is not what is perceived as the average businesswoman.

When it was suggested I mention her in this book, I was told this woman from a small Newfoundland town supported herself from a young age, putting herself through school and gaining the admiration of many along the way. She went to work on the boats at a time when it was something women just didn't do. Through courage and determination she developed her own niche.

With a B.Sc. in Honours Physics from Sir George Williams University (now Concordia) and a Masters of Science in Physical Oceanography from McGill University in hand, she was prevented from completing a Ph.D. on the physical oceanography of offshore Labrador by an injury at sea. Academic work behind her, Bobbitt undertook numerous research projects in her field, which led her to start her own environmental research company, Oceans Ltd., in 1981.

Oceans Ltd. was originally established as a means of providing physical oceanographic services to the fisheries and the offshore oil industry. Since that time, the company has grown and diversified substantially and is now a major provider of other offshore-related services, including marine weather forecasting, meteorology/climate studies, wind and wave extreme analysis, real-time three-dimensional iceberg profiling, environmental effects biomonitoring, and marine search and rescue research and development — with all service activities continuing the company's original premise of providing marine expertise in order to improve safety at sea. Oceans Ltd. remains based out of St. John's, but due to the growth of the offshore sector in Nova Scotia, the company now has a base of operations in Halifax, making the company truly Atlantic Canadian.

Judith Bobbitt has prepared numerous current analysis reports for various oil industry clients and established the environmental design criteria for the White Rose production platform. Her scientific work has been mainly in the area of ocean circulation on the Labrador Shelf and Grand Banks and estuarine circulations in bays and fjords. She has worked on the drift modelling of life rafts and the validation of CANSARP, a search and rescue drift model. She is currently working on environmental design criteria, characterization of icebergs, and ocean circulation on the Grand Banks and Flemish Pass.

Just goes to show — when the passion and determination are there, the possibilities are endless.

Chapter Three:
Networking, Mentoring, and the Sisterhood

Climb Aboard and we'll make our boats go faster!
Ann Price, Executive Director,
PEI Business Women's Association

A friend was reading a newspaper and commented on something she was reading. "This is neat, they describe female friendships as 'tend and befriend,'" she said. "What a nice way to put it."

The words stuck with me. Nice. And accurate. At least in my experience. Women support each other, inspiring courage to try new things and confidence in self. They understand our concerns and commitments to spouses and children. They often mirror each other in their interests and approaches. In my experience, women are not demanding and are open to talking about things one could never discuss with men — simply because of a different mindset.

If I go to my husband with a business worry, or perhaps feeling slighted by someone else's actions, he instantly goes into don't-mess-with-my-woman mode and wants to take charge of defending me and my honour. Love the man to death, but don't need him to take up arms on my behalf. What I need is not to be thrust into calming him, or his carrying on about righting the wrongs he perceives being done.

I just want to dump my feelings — to vent and to move on. I have been so fortunate in my life to have a network of women friends to hear me out when needed. Many, many times those gals have been my cheering section, my support group, and my salvation. I can phone them, rant for a few minutes, we laugh, and I've got my woes out of my system.

Spread across the country, I feel they are my kindred spirits. They are women whom I bounce ideas off, who urge me to go for it, and whom I value highly. They are not next door. In fact, only one of my magic circle lives in the same province. We often don't talk for months and see one another less, but when we do it's like we were never apart. I try to fulfill the same role for each and every one of them.

And this is only one aspect of sisterhood. Women in Business and professional organizations abound in Canada, providing wonderful support for those of us with an entrepreneurial soul.

One of the most important things you can do for yourself is to become part of a professional organization related to your work. The camaraderie, the information shared, the recognition of what you are doing, the sharing of common interests, all work together to create a bond and a network that can prove invaluable. It can be a source of education specific to your particular field or interest.

An organization can be one of the most important support factors in your working life. As in all things that are important, the decision about which group to join is one that requires some research and thought. It may even mean trying one or two before you find the group that works best for you.

To Join or Not to Join: That Is the Question, at Least for Today

It seems to happen as soon as you open for business — a proliferation of communications insisting that you *must* avail yourself of the services of various associations, organizations, groups, on-line services, and cooperatives.

Many who deem themselves vital to your survival are high profile: the chamber of commerce, board of trade, and merchants' association just for starters. Then there are those specific to your area of interest. It doesn't matter what you do, there are those vying for membership dollars. There are associations for women in business, home-based businesses, rural businesses, and city businesses ... it fair boggles the mind!

Ironically, finding the organization that best serves you can be a daunting proposition. For some, rubbing shoulders with their profession's superstars brings so much satisfaction that high fees in an elitist organization are worth every penny. Others have more business-specific needs: education, sourcing supplies, group insurance, marketing assistance, and so on. The benefits of belonging can be legion.

Along with the obvious is peer support, a connection that can be hard to maintain when you work in isolation. Before signing on the dotted line, research well and ask yourself the following questions:

How Do I Find the Group That Will Work for Me?
- Research what groups are available to you by asking your peers (word of mouth is the best way to find the best in anything), doing internet searches, checking with local organizations in your field, and checking with the government.
- Consider how the group can benefit you, whether there are educational opportunities (for example, do they have an annual conference with workshops that you normally would not have access to), whether membership will help to establish your credibility, and whether their membership directory or referral service could generate income.

What Are My Options?
- Ask others in your field for recommendations.
- What do they offer? (Costs, benefits, and so on.)
- Ask about members in your area, and references.
- Check out the membership requirements (if there are no requirements for professional credits, then the organization may not be as targeted as you would like).
- Ask for a newsletter, activities in your area, and directory.

What Do I Need? (Networking, peer support, education, listing in a directory or catalogue, discounts on merchandise or services, prestige, professional recognition, marketing information ...)

- Does this organization meet *my* needs?
- Exactly *what* do I get for my dollar?
- Do I *need* to join? (Some professions and have strict affiliation requirements before you can work.)
- What makes this organization better than others?
- Do they lobby or work toward things that influence my ability to make money?
- Are local meetings and educational opportunities available?
- Do the people and the policies of the organization please me? (You won't benefit if you don't feel comfortable.)
- Does my profession or trade benefit from the work done by this organization? (Don't overlook this one, it's important.)

Compare your needs with what each has to offer by making a table chart (a rough one is fine), then put your dollars where you determine you will get the best return. And remember: it's all useless if you don't get involved. Your association can be one of your greatest assets. Become a participant, a contributor, and the right organization will return dividends!

Culinary Diva: Kasey Wilson

In the early 1980s I was certain I had found something close to Utopia. Invited to do cooking demonstrations at a large consumer food show in Vancouver, I felt like a star. Airfare and a first-class hotel paid for, onstage presentations based on my book, radio and newspaper interviews: all combined to convince me I had made it. The reality was I was a very small player in a huge game, one of more than a dozen "celebrity" cooks. Even so, being part of the Viva Show was a big step. The experience did several things for me. It made me aware of the potential out there if I chose to pursue it. It gave me a sense of accomplishment, because I came to realize the value that others saw in what I did. But, most importantly, it introduced me to a kindred spirit, a sisterhood.

To set the scene ... The show was in BC Place, a new facility at the time; rather posh and impressive. There were several stages set up with ongoing cooking shows. Each attracted a large audience of up to two hundred. Samples of what you demonstrated had to be offered to everyone in the audience. I had it easy. I was cooking P.E.I. Mussels with a simple preparation. However, another cookbook author whose shows were close to mine was dealing with a more time-consuming and more difficult presentation. Kasey Wilson of Vancouver, author of *The Granville Island Cookbook*, was making truffles. Flavoured with Grand Marnier and a boysenberry liqueur, they were the hit of the show. The first evening I was doing cleanup in the behind the stage kitchen after my show. Working at another counter a beautiful, dark-haired woman was busily forming truffle after truffle. Just think about sheer numbers here. Everyone wanted to sample both, and some days Kasey was scheduled for more than one show. Next thing we knew I and another celebrity cook, Angela Clubb of *Mad About Muffins Cookbook* fame, were working alongside Kasey, gabbing, laughing, and making truffles. As we worked into the wee hours an instant bond was formed. Finally kicked out by security guards, we would chase down a late supper at a nearby "colourful" eatery before we moved to one of our hotel rooms and brainstormed — actually writing up concepts for future cookbooks for all three of us. Our creative energy was fuelled by chocolate truffles, muffins, mussels, and whatever samples we could garner from exhibitors. My last evening in Vancouver I went to Kasey's home for a party, ate more truffles, downed champagne, and cemented the bonds of a friendship that has endured for twenty years. My stomach wasn't sure we would survive the hours of the flight home — we had literally munched and slurped our way through five days of almost no sleep — but energy highs that have never since been equalled in my life kept me pumped for weeks.

Kasey's story was one that inspired me to pursue a freelance career. At that time I was still working full-time and was frankly scared to death of the idea of having no secure weekly paycheque. Her acceptance of my abilities, her enthusiasm for life on the edge, her quirky sense of humour, and her belief that we could achieve what we wanted by knuckling down and going for it fanned a flame that had been flickering in my soul. When I met Kasey, she was midway through a divorce, had two teenagers, and was striking out on her own without the safety net of being married to a professional. Kasey, a budding food writer, had been teaching cooking classes in her Kerrisdale kitchen (with a mirrored ceiling) and at the Granville Island Public Market. Although working hard and finding success, she had always been secure in the knowledge that her husband's income was providing for the family. Then, suddenly, it was gone and she was the wage earner. What she did have was ambition. She had talent. She knew where she wanted to go and had a darn good idea of things to do to get there. She, to put it in basic terms, had guts and determination. She also had a support group of friends, family, and a generous twin sister. Back then she described what she wanted. She wanted to be a good mom. She wanted to be self-sufficient and self-motivated. She wanted to savour the culinary and wine worlds, to write about them, and to be acknowledged for her successes. She wanted to travel the world. She wanted to be creative and adaptable. She wanted to strike a balance between the unorthodox and the conventional. She wanted acceptance for who she was.

Well, Kasey achieved all of those things, one step at a time. Like many of us she divides her time, diversifying to ensure a steady and secure lifestyle. Just look at where Kasey is today — and she does it all as a home-based business. She has co-hosted (with respected wine journalist Anthony Gismondi) a popular fast-paced live radio show called *The Best of Food and Wine* on CFUN for seven years. *The Best of Food and Wine* has broadcast on location from food and wine festivals in New York, Seattle, Banff, Victoria, and Whistler. The Restaurant Association of B.C. and the Yukon awarded her the Media-Person of the Year for Outstanding Reporting in the Field of Hospitality in 1996. She is editor of *Best Places Vancouver* (1993 to the present), and over the past decade she has been involved in a variety of food-related projects, including writing cookbooks: *Pacific Northwest the Beautiful Cookbook* (International Association of Culinary Professionals cookbook award nominee), *Gifts from the Kitchen*, *The Granville Island Cookbook*, *Done Like Dinner* (with Tiger Williams), and *Spirit and Style*. She is the B.C. contributor to *Best Places Northwest* and *Northwest Best Bargains* and writes a quarterly newsletter to international media for Tourism Vancouver. As a freelance writer, she is a regular contributor to *Wine Access* magazine, and her publication credits include *National Geographic Traveler*, the *Vancouver Sun*, the *Province, Vancouver Magazine, Seattle Weekly, Canadian Living, Luxury Magazine, Diversion, CityFood, Food Service and Hospitality, En Route*, and the *Zagat Restaurant Survey*.

It didn't just fall into her lap. Remember our plan! Kasey studied at LaVarenne in Paris, France, and with Julia Child in Napa, California. She attended cooking classes in India, Japan, Thailand, Hong Kong, France, Italy, and the United States. She judged the International Martini Challenge (in 1999 and 2000) and the Canadian Cookbook Awards (established in 1998). At the Vancouver Playhouse International Wine Festival in 1998, she was the only person to judge all three competitions: the Wine List Competition, the Fetzer Bonterra Appetizer, and the Dessert Awards. She has judged the National Bread Contest and the Jack Daniels Barbecue Cook-off, among others. Kasey has made several television and radio appearances and was featured on the PBS documentary *Cooking in the Beautiful Northwest*, a CNN documentary on Vancouver, and NBC's *Travel Secrets of the Pacific Northwest*. Kasey was B.C. director and chair of the board of Cuisine Canada in 1997, a board member of Les Dames d'Escoffier, and a board member of Canada à la Carte, a VQA wine and Canadian regional food promotion organization. In her off hours, she enjoys salmon fishing and looking for the perfect pinot noir. While she admits that many of the negotiations involved in getting good contract jobs can be "nerve wracking," she also takes pride in the fact that she puts effort into obtaining work that is good for her. "What I'm trying to do is stay focused on what I enjoy doing. I want time to matter when I'm accepting assignments now."

One thing that Kasey Wilson emphasizes is that throughout her career she has had such good support from both men and women. In fact, people have commented on how effectively she uses resources like industry contacts. "I've always maintained the most important thing to remember in life is 'to know what you don't know.' I'm a pretty good solution-oriented person so if I have an issue, I want to go to the professionals who are respected in their field. I've always found successful people are extremely generous with information and if you listen to their ideas, suggestions, and experiences, you'll be as effective they are.

"You have to be genuine and authentic. It's about relationship building so be someone others can trust. Maintaining a trusting relationship is easier than trying to win it back."

She also advises people to use their instincts and to listen to their gut. "I have a good BS detector (a flag goes up if I feel someone is telling me 'a story') and I have tried to learn to strategize a way of dealing with my concerns so I can grow.

"One thing I suggest chefs do before they open their restaurant is to write the review they would like to receive from a restaurant reviewer. Determine how you want to be thought about and talked about by your clients and prospective customers. What are the very best words they could use to describe you? People give back to their industries in many different ways. Rather than sitting on committees and attending meetings, I prefer to volunteer my time mentoring individuals and supporting their ideas."

Her sense of ethics and desire to give back have obviously worked well for this gal who is now billed as author, food editor, broadcaster, restaurant reviewer, and travel writer.

Radio Guest Tips

As a broadcaster who conducts hundreds of interviews, Kasey Wilson shares advice on how to be a great radio guest.

- In advance of your appearance, provide the host with a list of at least ten questions that you deem important or questions that you are frequently asked.
- Do not keep repeating the name and publisher of your book (if you are promoting your cookbook). Leave this for the host to do.
- Be a storyteller.
- Make the host laugh.
- Be authentic.
- Create context (example: Your grandma's macaroni and cheese is a lot more interesting that the concept of macaroni and cheese).
- Be passionate about your subject.

- Be willing to go where the host takes you, even if it does not relate specifically to your book, subject, product, etc.
- Be willing to improvise and to riff with the host.
- Treat every call as if it's the most important one you'll ever receive.
- Always assume that the audience is as smart as you are; you are simply more knowledgeable.
- Remember that you are a guest in the listener's home (or car).
- If you have good news (a recent nomination or award, for example), have that information written out and hand it to the host. Let the host be the one to relay the news to the public. Let the host shine the spotlight on you.
- If possible, feed the host, not as a bribe, but to disarm and engage him or her.
- Bring a tape and make your request to the producer for a copy *before* the interview begins.

Sister Act of Differing Kinds

The concept of sisterhood is one best exemplified by two real sisters, Cathy and Gretha Rose, who have been quoted as saying that they went into business for themselves because they thought it would be too challenging to work for others. Gretha says she just thinks she is "unemployable," while Cathy seconds, "We're just too independent." Truth is, these dynamic women had the drive and vision to do it their own way.

Smile Maker: Cathy Rose

The dynamic duo returned home to Prince Edward Island in 1983 and used expertise gained in Alberta to found Creative Esthetics Dental Lab Inc. The only commercial dental laboratory in the province, it manufactures custom-made orthodontic, prosthetic, and crown and bridge dental appliances.

By building on skills learned on the job in Calgary, they increased sales by 70 percent annually for the first seven years. Cathy, now the sole owner and president, has built Creative Esthetics to annual sales of $1 million and is moving into exporting. She employs a workforce of ten. Her business philosophy includes some great marketing strategies, and emphasis is on "servicing clients to death."

She takes pride in the fact that she helps people improve their lives both from a physical health aspect and as a maker of smiles. She has also had some fun elements with her business: building special "teeth" for occasions such as Halloween, working with pets, and even, she grins, working with hockey players.

Quite an achievement for someone who started a small laboratory to provide a living for herself and her daughter.

Cathy is a compulsive "doer" who is known for her contributions of time and energy to numerous good works. Despite the company's success, Cathy is still looking for new opportunities. The Canadian Young Entrepreneur and Atlantic Canadian Women Entrepreneur award winner attributes much of the company's success to the business environment on Prince Edward Island.

One of her commitments to give back to the community is her volunteer participation on many boards, including the IWK Health Centre (regional children's hospital), Tremploy, Charlottetown Chamber of Commerce, Junior Achievement, and several other national boards. She is the past president of the P.E.I. Women In Business Association.

Looking back, Cathy says, "One of the most important things when we started out was a babysitting cooperative. I couldn't have survived those first years without that."

Cathy Rose, Creative Esthetics Dental Lab Ltd., keeps her advice short and simple:

"Always follow your dreams, accepting that fear is your ever-present friend. Keep walking even if some days it seems like one step at a time. Life is too short to live small."

Filmmaker: Gretha Rose

And so we turn to sister Gretha Rose. After ten years with the dental lab, she was ready for a change. And change she got. Gretha is now the owner and president of Cellar Door Productions Inc., a production company that sells film and television shows worldwide with an annual production revenue ranging between $5 and $7 million.

Now operating from offices in the high-tech Atlantic Technology Centre in Charlottetown, Cellar Door took its name from the place where it was born. On a quiet street, in an upper-middle-class neighbourhood, a waterfront home gave no outward sign of the exciting things happening inside. A small, hand-lettered sign, "Deliveries to rear," led visitors through a gate, down garden steps, and around the patio to the entrance into Cellar Door Productions.

The home of Gretha Rose provided a private location for a creative and diverse company involved in "developing, financing and producing quality, value based animated and live-action productions with national and international partners in the areas of television series and feature films." In layman's terms, this is the birthplace of some great television series and specials.

The Inn Chef, a syndicated lifestyle cooking show capturing the energy of Chef Michael Smith, was followed by a second series, *Chef at Large*, and several specials. One food documentary, *Saturday Night, A Day in the Night of Chef Michael Smith*, was awarded the very prestigious Broadcast Media Award for Best National Television Cooking Show or Special during the James Beard Awards held in New York City. They are now producing a third food series.

Gretha and her crew also found success with animation. Their television special *The True Meaning of Crumbfest* tells the heart-warming Christmas story of a curious mouse named Eckhart. The show, rated as the best Christmas special of the year by BBC, sold to over twenty-seven countries and inspired *Eckhart: The Series*, celebrating the pioneering spirit, joys, and challenges of growing up in Prince Edward Island, exploring big themes and adventures from a very small perspective; it is shown on TeleTOON, in Canada. More recently, the animated short *Doodlez* was awarded the 2003 Gemini for Best Animated Program or Series.

"*Doodlez*, our animated series, has become so popular in its two-minute format that we are in the process of creating a long format series of half-hours. We are in negotiations with Warner Brothers and Cartoon Network in the US to come in as possible partners," Rose says.

"We are growing and evolving every day, it's hard to keep up with myself on certain days. We are expanding our existing properties to maximize their ancillary sales potential and to forward our existing television brands. We are beginning a new series with Chef Michael Smith entitled *Chef at Home.* We feel that this series, coupled with *The Inn Chef* and *Chef at Large,* allows us to begin to realize revenues from cookbooks, video deals, sponsorship entitlements, endorsement contracts, etc."

The Doc Series, commissioned by Global Television, gives viewers an in-depth look at one of North America's leading animal hospitals, Charlottetown's Atlantic Veterinary College at the University of P.E.I. As well, they have produced made-for-television movies, and they provide services to numerous projects.

These are just a sampling of the works of Cellar Door Productions. Pretty amazing for a woman who says she had no interest — had never dreamed nor aspired to — a career in filmmaking. An entrepreneur at heart, she was taking time to decide what to do after selling her half of the dental lab to her sister when a broken back forced her to spend hours lying flat on the couch.

She recalls, "I wanted something creative, using my business skills. I saw a program on the television industry in Nova Scotia and thought, that's it! I called people and came up with a concept for a movie ... It was a strange and wacky path followed. I wasn't really sure what I was doing."

But she quickly learned, developing properties or bodies of work. In the early days she utilized office space in her sister's building, but romance triggered change.

"We had decided to get married, to create a life. He'd come from Toronto where he worked eighteen-hour days — he wanted a change." She knew her business had a future, and more importantly knew she wanted a change of lifestyle.

"My children were six and nine. My dream had been to have a home office where the kids could walk home from school and I would be the first person to hear about their day."

As much as the move home was a good one, the move into television production has been a business success. Although the company has only been incorporated since 1996 they have established a film industry in Prince Edward Island.

"People think of it as being in the middle of nowhere. Life is perspective and in this business you get to have a lot of it. I look upon us as being halfway between Cannes and Hollywood. We are at the centre of the film industry; a worldwide business, very international."

It is, she states, "pretty amazing. Not only did I create a new business. Cellar Door is a new industry not known or embraced before in the province."

She could be the Canadian poster girl for the concept of developing successful partnerships. The provincial government has worked with her to develop policies and guidelines that are "Probably one of the best examples of public/private partnerships."

Rose says, "I'm still amazed that I did what I did. I could not not do this. I've done it all. Big company, big growth. Being married to the infrastructure, having to work very hard to pay big bills. Here I have freedom. It has allowed us great flexibility."

She also has the challenges that come with big budget productions It's all made possible by partnerships and co-interprovincial/internal production funding.

"I split the division of duties between myself and co-producers very carefully. It's a big commitment to stay small and work smart. We have a nice family atmosphere for the staff which ranges from 15 to 150 at any given time."

When word goes out that Cellar Door is going into pre-production they are contacted by up to 150 people a day: actors, musicians, technicians; all who work on a show.

"If production values get compromised I stop. I'm a stickler for quality and won't proceed. Others would but I won't. It's worked well. We are doing more than 95 percent of production companies in Canada do and we do it from here."

Scent of Spice Sweet Smell of Success: Karen Murray

A fascination with the business process led Karen Murray on a path to entrepreneurship that began with a business mentoring project offered by the Business Development Bank and a business women's organization and that resulted in the formation of Prince Edward Island Spice Merchants.

"My interest was learning how to — the business process, the plan," she recalls. Karen started as a home-based wholesale business in October 1996. She set her mind on research and solid preparation before launching her product, a line of gourmet spice and herb blends.

The quality and integrity behind the product have always been paramount. Murray orders from one of the highest quality importers in the country, and her early recipes were developed with consultation from the chef/owner of one of the most respected restaurants in the province.

"The product line developed slowly. It [the business] has grown steadily," she says, explaining that she has allowed herself development flexibility. "I haven't written anything in stone, if it grows at a fairly rapid rate, I'm prepared to grow with it."

Spice blending is done in a laboratory-like kitchen located in a corner of a garage, "with health department blessing. We let them know right from beginning what we were doing and followed their rules explicitly. It saved us a lot of money."

The Spice Merchants markets bottled gourmet spice blends. Other products, such as sea salt, are sealed in cello bags and packaged in small cloth sacks; gift packs hold an assortment, and she sells display cabinets to shops selling her products.

She is equipped to diversify from standard shaker-top bottles and cotton bags designed for consumer sales. The company can, for example, handle large orders for bulk blends and do custom blending for clients.

Challenges in the business are ongoing. Labelling, for example, involves finding the right technology — making sure the specs on quality of paper and glue are right. The blending process is also taxing because of the strong smell of spices, the need to wear a mask, and the physical strain. To start up she took out a new entrepreneurs loan, which was quickly paid.

"Shipping is my biggest expense," she says, explaining that it, in a way, represents why she feels involvement with the right organization is vital for small businesses.

"When I started out money was tight. I joined the P.E.I. Food and Beverage Processors Association rather than other organizations. It proved to be very helpful to me." She also joined Buy PEI, and has served on the board of both.

"The interaction with other members, large and small, has been phenomenal. In my wildest imagination I could never have imaged the support that would be there from the organization and its members.

"I gave a talk at the local community college and said no matter what you do, when you decide to take the step find people in similar business to support you. They share experience, time, in some cases, you can do business with them.

"I look to my organization to, in the future, work out something to counteract high shipping rates, maybe pull small companies together to combine shipping or something. Other small companies — lots of us — could benefit by getting better shipping rates."

Karen stresses that those things, as important as they are, are only the spinoffs from two very important functions of an industry association.

"If we as producers need to lobby government on particular issues the association is our vehicle for doing that as one voice. It also provides a learning environment for business, lunch and learn, workshops, conferences. These are very important advantages for small producers in particular."

With the support available through industry associations, her mentor, and agencies such as the Business Service Centre, Karen Murray has been able to enjoy the very facets of business that interested her from the beginning. And she's been able to do it at home.

She gave up a "high stress, administrative level job to go," she pauses in reflection, then grins, "find myself. I'm working longer hours, but it's for yourself and you are excited about what you are doing. As my son said you get to pick the eighteen hours you work a day."

Doing business with a home-based business often means meeting in the family kitchen rather than a more sterile office environment, something Murray finds a definite plus. "It's just great the people you meet. One of the nice things about a home-based business; you are working for yourself. It keeps you involved, in contact with people. Business is exciting — the creative juices start to run when I'm talking to like-minded people. Ideas, design — it gushes — it flows. I enjoy the highs — there are lows, certainly there are lows — but the high points are wonderful. They are your highs and lows not someone else's. Ideas just churn. Sometimes you can't sleep — there is so much exciting to think about."

The largest market for seasoning blends from P.E.I. Spice Merchants is local, with peak sales at Christmas and during the summer tourist season. However, she does sell product throughout the Maritimes, in Ontario, and in Quebec. While her main business remains wholesale, P.E.I. Spice Merchants attends some craft fairs, and she sells retail when requests come in the mail. She entered into a co-op mail-order catalogue with Seacroft, a mail-order company that focuses on Prince Edward Island culinary accessories such as spices and cookbooks.

When asked for her advice to other entrepreneurs, Karen Murray stressed the importance of doing a marketing plan. "You have to prove that market is there. You will save yourself a lot of trouble if you do." She also suggests utilizing the services of business service centres and, most importantly, says, "Have the desire to make the business work."

Mentoring

A few years back I had the good fortune to be involved in several federal government–sponsored mentoring programs. One program, directed to women wishing to develop a small business, teamed an experienced entrepreneur with someone in a start-up phase. Others were more focused, teaming writers specializing in particular areas or specialties with those seeking help and direction. In all cases the experienced individuals were compensated financially for their time. And in some both participants received a small grant to cover their costs and time.

The programs varied. Some were one-on-one; both participants were given opportunities to attend related workshops and events, and the whole group of mentors got together regularly to celebrate progress. Another was conducted totally by e-mail and involved a mentor and protégé who lived thousands of miles apart.

The beauty of mentoring is that it can be totally focused to a particular need. In my own case I have been a mentor to others at least a half-dozen times. I have also teamed up with someone who mentored me in an area where I felt I needed assistance.

These were the best programs for those hoping to pursue self-employment or small business. They gave the newbie a period of help that was focused directly on his or her needs. This one-on-one time is invaluable.

There is occasionally a question as to why mentors are financially compensated. The answer is simple. First and foremost they are being asked to take time away from their own business and to pass along expertise that they have spent years acquiring. Secondly, I very firmly believe that payment is a form of acknowledging the individual's worth. It sends the message that this person has a valuable contribution to make. Her knowledge, her willingness to share, and her ability to work with others are a reflection of her status in her field.

To constantly ask women to volunteer, to give away their services and their expertise, just reinforces the lack of respect and acceptance of them as professionals and experts in their chosen field.

Although, at this time, government-funded mentoring programs don't seem to be available, at least not in my province, there are other options. Many professional organizations have a mentoring program. As well, some private mentoring is available. To research programs in your area, first and foremost ask for them. Go to government agencies such as Human Resources Canada, go to organizations such as Women in Business associations. Those working in the arts can approach their arts organizations for funding for one-on-one mentor training.

On Mentoring and Networking

Two women I consider part of my sisterhood network are both proponents of seeking support and input from peers and of the benefits of mentoring. There is more on both of these women in chapter four, "From Quill to Keyboard." Consider:

Barbara Florio Graham

"I love 'the community of writers' that develops when I get involved in a writers' organization," says Barbara Florio Graham, author, freelance writer, and speaker, from Gatineau, Quebec. "This has been particularly satisfying in the Periodical Writers Association of Canada [PWAC], but that may be because I've been a member for twenty-five years. There is an exchange of ideas, opinions, advice, and personal anecdotes within the group, especially since we have an e-mail list. This organization, and one other that I belong to, provide wonderful support and encouragement to both beginners and the most experienced. I think networking is essential for freelancers. We work in isolation, and need to stay informed about current markets and trends, as well as to enlarge the number of contacts who may provide future work. I have one local friend who phones me whenever she needs writing advice, and I use her as my 'first editor' for certain pieces when I want to make sure I'm engaging the reader sufficiently."

Ann Douglas

On joining: "Some people operate on the mistaken assumption that they'll put themselves at a competitive disadvantage if they network with others in their profession. I've found that quite the opposite is true. There's more than enough work to go around, and if everyone is generous about sharing leads and swapping tips on working smarter, everyone benefits and everyone's business grows. It's a case of switching your mindset from one of competition to one of cooperation: of realizing that working cooperatively not only feels good — it makes solid business sense."

On mentoring: "I was fortunate enough to be able to take advantage of the Periodical Writers Association of Canada's mentorship program at the very point in my career when I was ready to make the leap from writing for magazine and newspapers to writing books. [She now has twenty-seven, many of them best-sellers.] I was paired up with an experienced author who was able to coach me through the process of writing my first book proposal and negotiating my first book contract. I've been able to apply what I learned many times since and am now mentoring other writers through the process of landing that elusive first book contract."

Mentor Wanted: Finding the Perfect Partner

Before you begin the search for a mentor, take the time to nail down exactly what you want help with now. Mentoring is not about developing an ongoing relationship (as girlfriends are wont to do), but rather about developing the mentality of using mentoring as a method of learning specific things from someone knowledgeable in that area, and then turning to someone else with different knowledge or expertise when another need arises. So, before seeking a mentor, put yourself in control:

- Do an assessment of what your needs are. What do you need assistance with? What skills do you need to work on?
- Do an assessment of how quickly you want to see results. What time frame are you working with? Would a short, say two weeks or a month, relationship work, or are you looking for a longer term commitment?
- Think about who would be the perfect mentor and do some research to detail people you feel would offer you what need. Are these people available to you? Where can you find others with similar things to contribute?
- Set out the terms you feel would work. How much time and how frequently would you like to work with your mentor? What are your expectations? How much are your willing to contribute financially? Are there funding alternatives?
- Bring an agenda that is tied to your goals to your potential mentor. How will you structure your sessions, as informal meetings or more structured teaching? Do you want general advice, or someone willing to delve into your business or your books?

> • Remember, you don't need a single mentor for life, so tailor short-term goals accordingly.
>
> Once you have fine-tuned your aspirations, the search for the perfect mentor can begin.

Healing Journey Culminates in Life Design: Lekha Shan

Lekha Shan, former president of the Vancouver Island Women's Business Network, has developed a business around helping people find mind/body solutions for success and wellness through her Victoria company, Life Design Unlimited.

The certified hypnotherapist and Neuro-Lingustic Programming practitioner holds a diploma from the Faculty of Astrological Studies in the U.K. and is a Trainer of the Psychology of Vision, a graduate of Anthony Robbins's Mastery University, and a practitioner of Mind/Body Harmony and Raindrop Therapy. She says the different fields have given her a balance in how she looks at the world and how she works with people. She finds it both stimulating and challenging, and it encourages her to constantly search for better, easier, and more effective ways to help.

Lekha, of East Indian origin, came to Canada almost ten years ago from Europe. She was visiting a friend in Victoria when "extreme strong intuition — an inner whisper" told her this was where she was meant to be. The feeling remained strong, so after three months back in Paris, she packed her bags and moved to Canada.

"I lived in the U.K. for many years and was divorced almost twenty years ago. I had to overcome the social stigma of divorce, heal my wounds, learn a profession (having never worked before), heal my relationships with my children and discover who I was underneath all the cultural/societal 'conditioning.' My own healing journey led me to discover my passion and my potential."

What I learned and practiced on myself became the tools I use to help others follow their passions by helping them discover who they are behind the masks they wear and helping them overcome the obstacles such as fear of failure, lack of self-esteem, lack of confidence, self-sabotage, by using a whole variety of tools and techniques."

She has spent the past eighteen years exploring and learning many aspects of personal growth and self-knowledge and has been working with an international clientele for the past fourteen years, giving telephone consultations.

Lekha says, "When you start living who you truly are, people start to really respect you. As you heal, your relationship with everything around you changes." In business and in private life, change is inevitable — and often desirable. "If we're not continually evolving, it affects everyone around us. It's like we have to eat every day, drink every day. We always have to learn about ourselves and grow. As a Chinese saying goes: 'When someone shares something of value, and you derive benefit from it, you have an obligation to share it with others.' This ensures that there is a constant flow of positive things given and received in the world."

Chapter Four:
From Quill to Keyboard

Make sure you're totally passionate about the type of work you choose because you're going to invest a lot of time and effort into growing your business. Ideally, you want to choose a line of work that feels like something you were put on the planet to do and that helps to make the world a better place. There's more to being in business than just making a living, after all.

Ann Douglas

One profession where women have always excelled, and have done a huge service by recording social history and life from a female perspective, is writing. It is accessible, because it can be accomplished with no expensive education or specialized equipment and can be done almost anywhere; it provides a passageway through doors that would otherwise have been closed. It has opened eyes and acknowledged the feminine viewpoint of all manner of things.

Have to admit to sneaking this chapter in on my publisher. It had originally been my intent to drop women writers in throughout the text of the book. Writers are, after all, a vital component of my life — they are my inspiration, my colleagues, my peers, and most importantly my friends. They are also responsible for recording the accomplishments of women throughout Canadian history and weaving the stories which I so love reading.

However, opportunities presented by mastering the written word have been so important to women that I decided to devote a chapter to those who earn their living through the brain-to-fingers process that we call writing. After all, J.K. Rowling penned her way to riches greater than those of Queen Elizabeth II with her Harry Potter adventures. Writing took her from status as a single mother living on welfare to an enormous fortune.

And look at our own history. The Famous Five — the women who struggled to have women declared "persons" so they could be appointed to the Canadian Senate — all used the power of the written and spoken word. Individually, each was a prominent women's leader in her own right; together, Emily Murphy, Henrietta Muir Edwards, Louise McKinney, Irene Parlby, and Nellie McClung were a force that changed history. Nellie McClung, lecturer, teacher, and writer, used voice and pen to battle for the suffragette and temperance movements. McClung was also a novelist and politician of note. Judge Emily Murphy, the first woman police magistrate in Edmonton, used both articles and books to bring attention to such important issues as drug trafficking. We could write a whole book about the contributions and talents of these women alone.

There is also the fact that writing and teaching are natural spinoffs from many other activities. Gardeners, for example, often end up writing books, as do chefs and cooks. Many entrepreneurs are asked to give workshops and develop manuals or handout materials, later developing these into magazine articles or books. Writing a book about one's experiences is, after all, the crowning glory for many careers.

Some of our earliest acknowledged women achievers were writers. This was deemed an acceptable thing for a woman to do in the days of first settlement. Writing has proved a means of independence for women for hundreds of years and continues to be so. One of the best things about this as a profession is that it's not dated in any way. I know numerous writers who began at various stages of life and continued writing into their eighties and later.

They write single, married, divorced, widowed, with children or grandchildren and without.

They wrote with lead pencils in journals as they walked and rode wagons to settle the west. They write on laptop computers as they travel in RVs or on desktop computers as they look out on raging Maritime snowstorms.

While we can't possibly include all of the great Canadian writers here, we can look at a few of my favourites, and also sample the diverse work available, even within this one career choice. This is just a sampling of how many spins can be taken on just one skill area.

Way Back Then: Catharine Parr Traill and Susanna Moodie

Two early writers, sisters Catharine Parr Traill and Susanna Moodie, emigrated from England in the early nineteenth century to take up residence in Ontario. These literary sisters left a rich record of life in Upper Canada (Ontario these days). Catherine left a clear record of what it was like to tramp through the bush north of Lake Ontario and create a life and home from scratch in her books *The Backwoods of Canada* and *The Female Emigrant's Guide* (later retitled *The Canadian Settler's Guide*).

Gardens in Print Then and Now: Marjorie Harris and Carol Martin

Annie L. Jack was one of the early garden columnists, writing "Garden Talks" for the *Montreal Daily Witness*, and in 1903 the column led to a book, *The Canadian Garden: A Pocket Help for the Amateur*. *The Canadian Garden Book*, 1918, by Adele H. Austen (writing under the pseudonym Dorothy Perkins) was the second book of gardening advice published by a Canadian.

Today we have another star in the world of garden writing. Marjorie Harris of Toronto has written an astonishing number of books on the subject, edits a gardening publication, and is a regular columnist, according to *The History of Canadian Gardening*. A trip to her web site and a read about her life is a true inspiration as it details challenges met and opportunities seized.

When Carol Martin was freelancing in the 1990s, part of her work involved organizing exhibitions for the National Library of Canada, something she describes as "wonderfully interesting work that took advantage of [her] lifelong interest in books and publishing." Since Canadian publishers were beginning to publish a broad array of gardening books, she suggested an exhibition on the subject, and the library agreed.

Carol followed one of the golden rules of freelancing, whether as a writer or as something else. She came up with an idea, presented it to her client, and they brought it. Quite often an original or new idea presented to a potential client will result in a contract. I've done the same thing with promotions, brochures, and such.

Now Carol knew there were enough new books to make an interesting display, and there was enough interest to attract an audience. What she didn't know was how fascinating a historical subject she had chosen, as there was little Canadian information published.

When she began researching for the exhibition, two resources were particularly helpful. One was the pioneering work on the subject done by Edwinna von Baeyer, who wrote not only *Rhetoric and Roses: A History of Canadian Gardening 1900–1930*, but also the invaluable *A Selected Bibliography for Garden History in Canada*. The other was the work of landscape historian Pleasance Crawford. The two women edited a book together, *Garden Voices: Two Centuries of Canadian Garden Writing*.

"The more research I undertook for the exhibition, the more fascinated I became with how a study of Canada's garden history opened up a unique view of the country's social history," she says. She decided to continue her study and eventually wrote her own book, *A History of Canadian Gardening*, published by McArthur & Company of Toronto in 2000. The book is a wonderful read for anyone interested in gardens, nature history, and household history.

It is also typical of the evolution of an interest or project. The exhibition, "Cultivating Canadian Gardens: The History of Gardening in Canada," ran for most of 1998 and is still available on the library's web site.

Wordsmithing Rancher: Sharon Butala

Sharon Butala was born and educated in Saskatchewan. She moved from Saskatoon to Eastend after marrying a rancher in 1976. Sharon gave up work as a special educator to become a writer of novels, short stories, and creative non-fiction. She began writing as she struggled to cope with integrating into her new and strange environment, creating fiction that is credited with bringing the people and the landscape of the rugged Cypress Hills area of Saskatchewan to world literature. She took writing classes and credits the Saskatchewan Writers Guild for helping her to develop as a writer. Eventually she and her husband, Peter, agreed that her writing was more important than her active role doing ranch things like driving tractors, putting food by, and delivering calves. While she says she envied those who found contentment in such things, she concentrated on her award-winning fiction, adding such non-fiction topics as the crisis facing the rural community. Her book *The Perfection of the Morning* reached number one on the best-seller list in July 1994. And today she has an impressive list of credits, including *The Middle of Nowhere — Rediscovering Saskatchewan*.

Teacher, Writer, Teacher: Barbara Florio Graham

Many people get into writing as a sideline after finding success in another field. Barbara (Bobbi) Florio Graham found success as a writer and then fell back onto skills honed in a former profession so that she can diversify her way to financial stability. Her career development is a perfect example of how a career builds on steps taken along the way.

An author, teacher, and consultant (operating as Simon Teakettle Ink, with a wide range of clients), her publication credits range from books and articles on writing and publicity to humour, poetry, and articles about everything from how to train your cat to effective ways to handle the media. The former high-school teacher now teaches primarily on-line, with the occasional workshop or seminar. Her consulting clients include writers, self-publishers, non-profit organizations, and owners of small businesses.

Writing came naturally to this resident of Gatineau, Quebec, and she quickly began building writing credits.

"I think I've always been a writer. I was first published at the age of nine (in a children's magazine who paid me $5), and decided at eleven that I wanted to study journalism. I won contests for various types of writing while I was in elementary and high school, and served as one of the editors of my high school newspaper as well as the editor of the literary magazine." At university, part-time work at the public relations office provided experience writing press releases, and work at the college radio station led to her adapting and directing radio dramas. She also began her freelance career, writing how-to booklets (on everything from heart disease to the importance of vacations) for a small publishing company that sold them in bulk to industries, for staff lounges, lunchrooms, and waiting rooms. "During the time I held full-time teaching positions in both New York and Chicago, I took on freelance assignments in both writing and public relations, so going freelance on a full-time basis seemed natural after I moved to Canada in 1967." Freelancing is always a challenge, she says. "Each time you think you have all your ducks in a row, one or more of them is shot down as you watch! I've had regular jobs with local magazines or newspapers evaporate when the magazine was sold or the paper folded. I learned, finally, that diversification was the only survival strategy, and began to teach and do p.r. consulting in addition to writing." Her freelance career has brought many best, and worst, moments. "I used to get a thrill each time I saw an article of mine in print. Surely the highlight was the launching of my first book. *Five Fast Steps to Better Writing* was launched at Ottawa City Hall, and received a rave review in the *Ottawa Citizen*. I felt on top of the world! More recently, I've been most excited at the accomplishments of other writers I've mentored. I continue to hear from many former students, both from my days teaching high school in Chicago and from those I've mentored over the past decade."

Of course the good is often tempered with the bad, and she says her worst moments have been when a publication has let her down, either by stringing her along with promises of publication only to renege at the last minute or by delaying payment. "It doesn't matter how valid their reasons are — change of editor, change of focus, parent company selling the magazine, sudden financial woes — it's always disturbing to know that writers are at the bottom of the food chain when these things occur."

Like most individuals who freelance for a living, Bobbi, looks to the future with eager anticipation. "One exciting aspect of freelancing is that you never know what the future will hold. I try to remain flexible, even as I make sure I reach certain goals. I'd like to complete a series of linked short stories I've been toying with for a while, so that may be my next book!"

Author, teacher, and consultant Bobbi Florio Graham, of Simon Teakettle Ink, shares her advice with those wishing to freelance.

"Every business needs a business plan. It has to be flexible, but you must set specific goals and timelines. It's also vital to keep excellent records, not only tracking income and expenses for tax purposes, but also tracking submissions and queries, so you can determine your best and worst prospects. Some freelancers work for the same publications for many years, spending time for a tiny fraction of their annual income that would be better spent pursuing newer, better markets. I also think it's important to diversify. It's dangerous to limit your fields of interest too narrowly, and foolish not to consider what else you might be able to do with expertise you've developed, research and interviews, and other raw material you accumulate for a particular assignment or project. Before moving on to something completely different, you have to investigate how you might exploit these in other ways. I believe one should consider 'recycling' before starting a new project, so you can gather sufficient material to sell many different articles, many times. Educating yourself about copyright and contracts is also essential!"

So, she says, is always being ready to promote and take pride in who you are and what you do. "I never go anywhere without brochures and bookmarks to hand out, as you never know who you may meet in an unlikely situation. I spoke to someone after a funeral who had heard about my cat but couldn't find *Mewsings* in her town. And I handed a bookmark to a man ahead of me in the grocery store recently. He was buying cat food and we started to chat ..."

(For Bobbi's take on networking see chapter three, "Networking, Mentoring, and the Sisterhood.")

Motherhood — A Passion and Career: Ann Douglas

Ann Douglas of Peterborough, Ontario, is a superstar in the world of pregnancy and parenting writing. Working under the business name Page One Productions Inc., this author, who also speaks and consults on parenting, has twenty-seven books and so many periodical and web publishing credits that we can't possibly list them.

Like many successful people, she built her credits and constantly strove to move up the ladder to reach her goals.

"I started writing for the local community newspaper when I was in high school. Then, when I hit university, I wrote for the university newspaper. After I graduated, I worked full-time for a software manufacturer (I wrote software manuals) and a community newspaper before taking the plunge and deciding to become a full-time freelance writer. That was ten years and four kids ago and I've never looked back."

The move into writing about pregnancy and parenting was a natural one for this devoted mom.

Ann had written extensively on parenting-related topics for magazines and newspapers and made the transition to writing books in 1997. As well as writing books and continuing to appear in print media, she now does a lot of corporate writing for the parenting market. For example, she wrote a series of ads for GM Montana minivans and writes Sunlight laundry detergent's GoAheadGetDirty Club newsletter. She is in demand as a speaker and does spokesperson work as well, appearing on a Cheerios box for the second time as part of a special campaign.

"I have a passion for writing about pregnancy/parenting," she confirms. "I generally spend about three months writing a book — sometimes a little less, sometimes a little more. When I'm on a roll, I can research and write about five thousand words per day. *The Unofficial Guide to Having A Baby* practically wrote itself because I was so passionate about the subject matter. There were times when I just put my fingers on the keyboard and waited to see what would come out.

"What I didn't realize until after my first book was published, however, is that an author's job doesn't really begin until after publication. If you want your books to do well, you have to put a huge number of hours into promoting them.

"I'm extremely good at juggling! I'm constantly switching from 'mother mode' to 'writer mode' in order to juggle the demands of my family and my career."

Ann has often wowed fellow writers with her ability to schedule writing time around her children's school and husband's work schedules. While she doesn't usually suffer from the complaint known as "writer's block" she does admit to occasionally struggling with a mild burnout, especially when working around the clock trying to meet a deadline.

"My brain has learned how to take care of itself, however, and will simply refuse to do anything more taxing than writing e-mail if I've been putting in too many hours on heavy-duty writing projects."

Motherhood has had a profound effect on Ann's life. "I can hardly remember what my life was like before I became a mother. I know I was once a single person who went to university and liked to spend her spare time reading novels, but it seems like the Ann who did those things was someone other than me!

"Becoming a mother has affected every area of my life. I've grown both personally and professionally. My children have taught me to be patient and tolerant and to go after my dreams.

"Before I became a mother, I couldn't think of anything meaningful to write about. Now, my children provide me with endless inspiration."

She says moms aspiring to write should take advantage of every stolen moment. It's advice any home-based mom should follow.

"If you can't get to your keyboard because you're trying to keep your toddler from doing backflips off the kitchen table, jot down your ideas on the back of a scrap of paper and tuck that scrap of paper in your pocket. Then, when you find yourself with the luxury of an hour or two of writing time, you can get right down to business: you'll already know what you want to write about.

"Connect with other moms who write. They can both support and inspire you. You can talk to them about what it's like to be so worried about your one-year-old's ear infection that you can't get any work done — or to be so caught up in the book that you're writing that you don't hear your child ask for a drink of juice until she's repeated her request a dozen times or more!

"Realize that being a writer is both a privilege and a responsibility. You have the best job in the world because you can research and write about things that matter to you, but you owe it to others to make the world a better place through your writing."

This diva of the baby and child world faced her challenges along the way. One was breaking through the barrier of getting acceptance that she had the talent and knowledge to do what she does, to get past the image of being "just a mom."

"I had a literary agent tell me I'd never be able to write for the parenting market because I didn't have a medical degree or a degree in psychology. Now my Mother of All books are available in Canada, the U.S., Russia, China, and Korea and well over a quarter million books of this series have been sold."

The books are well on their way to becoming pop culture pregnancy icons: one showed up on an episode of the very popular Dr. Phil television show (it was on the dresser of a pregnant teenager in an episode) and another on an episode of the cult classic *Six Feet Under*. She has endured "worst" moments, but always tempered by "bests."

The worst: "Having an editor leave a publishing company when she was about to make me an offer on my first book. The new editor wasn't interested, and my project died at that point. I was devastated."

The best: "Having my Mother of All books selling so successfully in the U.S. market. They are consistent top-sellers in the pregnancy/parenting category at Amazon.com and in standard retail channels."

And wait, there is more from this energized woman.

"Because of the nature of my work, I'm frequently asked to review products for moms and babies — great products that every mom should know about. I decided to pull some of the truly crème de la crème of mom and baby products together and produce my very own mail-order catalogue. Voilà! A catalogue is born ... *Mail Order Mama* is a division of Page One Productions Inc. Mail Order Mama.com is the first mail-order catalogue for the truly discriminating mama and mama-to-be. This catalogue

Ann Douglas says anyone starting, or in, business needs to be sure of one thing: "Make sure you're totally passionate about the type of work you choose because you're going to invest a lot of time and effort into growing your business. Ideally, you want to choose a line of work that feels like something you were put on the planet to do and that helps to make the world a better place. There's more to being in business than just making a living, after all."

is filled with products that are designed to nurture and pamper you during this special time in your life and encourage you to celebrate the amazing transition to motherhood: mom and baby herbal products, comfort kits for labouring women and new moms, pregnancy books, baby books, parenting books, children's books, songs about motherhood."

Seizing a Whole Lot of Romance: Bobby Hutchinson

One writer whose books I never pass by in a store is Bobby Hutchinson. For starters, she sets her contemporary romances in British Columbia, a region I love. Aside from that I enjoy the stories she weaves. So I went surfing on the web and found the Harlequin web site, eHARLEQUIN.com; on it was Bobby's story.

Born in small town in the interior of British Columbia, the daughter of a coal-mining father and housewife mother (both storytellers), she says learning to read was the most significant event of her early life.

Married young, with three sons, she says the middle child, who was deaf, taught her patience. Divorced after twelve years, she worked a variety of odd jobs: directing traffic at construction sites; providing daycare for challenged children; and selling fabric by the pound at a remnant store.

Mortgaging her house to purchase the remnant store, she began to sew — one dress a day. "The dresses sold, but the fabric did not, so she hired four seamstresses and turned the old remnant store into a boutique. After twelve successful years, Bobby sold the business and decided to run a marathon."

Training bored her, so she made up a story about Pheiddipedes, the first marathoner, as she ran. She wrote it down, sent it to *Chatelaine* magazine's short story contest, won first prize, and became a writer.

"Bobby remarried and divorced again, writing all the while. Today, she has thirty-five published books, and, currently, is working on three or four more. She has four enchanting grandchildren and lives alone. Bobby runs, swims, does yoga, meditates, and likes this quote by Dolly Parton: 'Decide who you are, and then do it on purpose.'"

What does she love most about being a writer? "Turning straw into gold — taking a tiny thread and making it into an entire imaginary world."

Bobby Hutchinson's advice is, of course, directed at writers, but can be applied to anything you want to pursue: "Visualize. See the book in print, imagine how it feels for you to be published, know that you are a wonderful writer. See yourself getting a fat check."

Words of wisdom: When asked who she admires and why, Bobby said, "My female friends. They persevere through the toughest, most incredible life changes, always with courage, and always looking for ways to help one another." She wears one diamond stud in her left ear, to remind herself that no matter how far she's come, she's only halfway.

Travel and Romance For a Grand Life: Sandra Field

I first met the writer you all know as Sandra Field in Prince Edward Island when she came to give a presentation on writing a romance novel. She inspired me that day. Oh, I do dream of writing romance novels. I'm not at that stage in my plan yet, but she inspired me to know that I could pursue this concept of changing from a dead-end job to an independent career as a writer — to being in charge of my own daily routine and my destiny.

She had left Prince Edward Island by the time we met and was pursuing a career as a romance writer in Nova Scotia. When we first met I think she had perhaps three novels to her credit. Today the number is over fifty. Her dream, she said, was to travel and set her books in many locales around the world.

She asked me a what-if question that gave me the courage to change. "What if," she said, "you stay where you are?" Some twenty years later I see others who have stayed where I was, working in the same newsroom. Oh, salaries have gone up a bit — not much, but a bit. They have had the security of a regular paycheque and benefits. But, from my perspective, they have missed so much. Their days have the same "sameness" that they had for me twenty years ago.

When I look back over my adventures of the past twenty years, I am so glad to have taken a chance on following my dream. So thanks J.M. — or Sandra — for the great gift of discovery.

According to eHARLEQUIN.com: "How did Sandra Field change from being a science graduate working on metal-induced rancidity of cod fillets at the Fisheries Research Board to being the author of over fifty Harlequins? When her husband joined the armed forces as a chaplain, they moved three times in the first eighteen months. The last move was to Prince Edward Island. By then her children were in school; she couldn't get a job; and at the local bridge club, she kept forgetting not to trump her partner's ace.

"However, Sandra had always loved to read, fascinated by the lure of being drawn into the other world of the story. So one day she bought a dozen Harlequin novels, read and analyzed them, then sat down and wrote one (she believes she's the first North American to write for Harlequin Romance).

"Her first book, typed with four fingers, was published as *To Trust My Love*; her pseudonym was an attempt to prevent the congregation from finding out what the chaplain's wife was up to in her spare time.

"She's been very fortunate to be able to combine a love of travel (particularly to the north — she doesn't do heat well) with her writing, by describing settings that most people will probably never visit. And there's always the challenge of making the heroine's long underwear sound romantic.

"She's lived most of her life in the Maritimes of Canada, within reach of the sea. Kayaking and canoeing, hiking and gardening, listening to music and reading are all sources of great pleasure. But best of all are good friends, some going back to high-school days, and her family. She has a beautiful daughter-in-law and the two most delightful, handsome, and intelligent grandchildren in the world (of course!)."

What does she love most about being a writer? "The freedom to choose my own hours. The fun of keeping eyes and ears open for new ideas." And what does she like least? "Finding one of my titles in a second-hand bookstore!"

What one specific piece of advice would she give a would-be writer trying to kick-start a career? "Read, read, read …"

One Job Title but Many Hats: Sandra Phinney

Another Atlantic Canadian who followed a different path to work with words was my good friend Sandra Phinney. Sandra is one of my role models. I truly admire the way she took life by the horns, set off in a new direction, and in just a short time wowed those who know her with her success, not only financial but also in finding a lifestyle where she excels. Not only is she successful, she also gives back, over and over and over again, offering advice, assistance, pats on the back, and moral support. Sandra may not know it, but she is one of the individuals I consider part of my sisterhood network — a valued and treasured element in my life.

I first met Sandra during a great weekend writers' conference at White Point Beach Lodge in southern Nova Scotia. I was giving workshops, one of them a version of the planning that we discussed in "Beginning With the Plan." When we breakfasted together knew I had met a kindred spirit.

Sandra is a freelance writer based in Yarmouth, Nova Scotia. One job title but many hats! She writes magazine articles spanning the worlds of business, science, health and fitness, farming and aquaculture, aerospace, outdoor, travel, and tourism, to name a few. She also creates short documentaries for CBC radio; manages projects; writes advertorial copy, brochures, and web content for corporate, NGO, and government clients; teaches freelance and creative writing workshops; delivers networking and marketing seminars for small business owners; and does the occasional gig as a keynote speaker. Recently she's ventured into the world of videos, writing scripts for a company that creates various productions, and she researches and writes backgrounders for some television shows. So how did she build such impressive credentials? Sandra tells her own story:

"I was fifty-four, a heartbeat away from bankruptcy, and needed income to feed a farm debt. (We had grown organic fruit and vegetables commercially for fifteen years but it was a huge financial drain. We stopped farming but I needed work to keep feeding the farm debt until we could find a buyer for the home and property.)

"As a pastime I used to write poetry and in the fall of 1998, attended a writer's workshop. There were many workshops covering different writing genres, including one titled something like 'Earning a Living as a Freelance Writer,' given by Julie Watson. I was smitten. Came home and told my husband that I was going to be a freelance writer and thought I could figure it out within six months. He smiled, and said 'Sounds like a plan!' but inwardly he thought I was a little looped."

When I asked Sandra why she followed the life of a freelancer (rather than seeking employment), she responded with passion.

"I love working for myself. Always have. With forty years in the workforce, I've often worked for others (taught school, did social work, managed a government office ... also did short-term jobs like waitressing and cutting fish) but I was never really happy working for others. Often loved the actual work but found that the bureaucracy was truly crazy-making and in some cases downright soul destroying.

"My work years that gave me the greatest job satisfaction and reward were the years I was self-employed. First as a retail store owner, then as a farmer, and now as a freelance writer. I'm fairly 'driven' so I can set high expectations and meet them. I also love the total independence and all the built-in 'choices' that are inherent in the job when you work for yourself."

Don't think it was an easy road for her to just suddenly become a writer; she faced the same challenge that many of us do, a lack of education or training in the specific field.

"I didn't have a degree in journalism or a masters in creative writing, so I had to figure out how to proceed and pick up skills in a hurry. I did this in a number of ways. I joined the Periodical Writer's Association of Canada as soon as I could and started to network, and get involved in the writing community. I looked for and found a mentor ... retired journalism professor who agreed to meet with me once a month. I sought out and took as many writing-related workshops as I could afford in the first couple of years. I bought many second hand-books on writing and editing, and read, read, read.

"My best moments are when I've discovered the 'story' within the story or assignment I'm working on ... it's like a 'eureka' moment ... and the magic that happens when the words flow and the story unfolds effortlessly. This is not an everyday occurrence. Mostly it's slugging away. But there are also some gem-like moments when the interview is electric and you get quotes and insights that are priceless. Or when you land an assignment that you've only been able to dream about. Or when someone calls you to say how much they enjoyed reading an article you've written. There are many, many 'best moments' in this field. And I've learned an incredible amount of things that I would never have known about!"

On the other side of the coin there are always "worst" moments! Like all people who have overcome these moments, Sandra talks about them with a sense of almost, well, glee. Because she had those worst moments, but she coped.

"Taping over an interview that I did for a CBC mini documentary. I had to travel back to the site and redo the whole thing. Took me two extra days and almost two hundred extra miles of travel," she recalls. "Discovering that I had two dead batteries in my camera while on a photo shoot in an isolated area in the middle of the province. I had to

Sandra Phinney has some advice and tips for others starting, or in, business:

- Set goals. They can always change, but you really need some kind of road map. Set not only business goals, such as how much income you plan to generate and where your sales are going to come from, but also goals for personal and professional development. Doing a skills inventory is a good place to start, then figure out what you'd like to be able to do really well and figure out ways and means to do just that.
- Never say no to a request. Although it sounds trite and clichéd, "where there's a will, there's a way" has proven solid and true over and over again.
- Be willing to try something new, whether you know how to do it or not. Might be scary, but you will learn and get better at it as time goes on. Proceed in spite of being afraid of making a mistake.
- Share market information and business tips ... network, network, network. Find like-minded spirits in the business world and make a point to take the time to communicate and nurture friendships.
- Be brave. Be honest. Be audacious. Be humble. Be the best that you can be.

travel sixty miles to get new batteries. Had my fairly expensive camera short out on me due to severe moisture conditions while touring in Belize. It was the second day of a ten-day journey and not only was I without my camera, I could not get it fixed anywhere in the country."

Her enjoyment of her chosen profession is reflected in her thoughts on the future. "I reckon I'll never live long enough to write all the stories I want to write ... and today is as exciting for me as the first day I started. I have a lot more confidence as a writer, but there is so much more to learn! I have started to do some travel writing, and just wrote a book. I hope to take more time to delve more into the worlds of fiction and poetry. Also photography. And longer documentaries. And script writing for film." And the list goes on!

Syndication Paves Road to Success: Cheryll Gillespie

Every so often we meet someone who breaks all the rules, ignores the tried and true, rushes in where no experienced person would, and manages to not just pull it off but to succeed well beyond what many can only imagine.

One such individual is Cheryll Gillespie, Canada's Design Diva, famous for her creative verve and magnetic approach to home fashion. Cheryll's star is rising in the enormously popular home design genre of television, radio, print, and personal appearances.

If you had asked teachers or parents if Cheryll would become a writer they would have said no chance. Her grade four report card said, "If Cheryll stopped talking she would make a great student."

An interior decorator by trade, she got bored. When an opportunity to work as field reporter for a television show presented itself, she jumped at it.

"I've been all over Alberta. It gave me oodles of TV experience in a short time. I loved it."

Soon, the woman who as a child "went to speech therapy for years" started thinking radio. At about the same time, she was asked to speak at a home and garden trade show. A home editor wanted to do a story on Cheryll. "I said okay, but I want to do a story for you."

The Canoe web site approached her about doing home and garden stories for them.

"I started thinking if ... if Ann Landers gets $5 for each article, but sells 20,000 that makes ...! Well it makes sense, if I was going to write one article, to have it appear in as many magazines and newspapers as I could."

And she did. Cheryll has established herself as a self-syndicated columnist — something most writers only dream of. Her nationally syndicated "Design and Décor" column is published weekly throughout North America and in the *Sun* chain of newspapers as well as on-line at www.canoe.ca. She is a regular contributor to many home improvement and entertaining publications with articles and decor advice appearing in magazines such as *Country Sampler* and *Leisureway's*.

Cheryll's television work continues with weekly home trends, newscasts, talk shows, television commercials, and guest appearances on a variety of news and talk programs. She's a regular on radio with "Interiors By Cheryll" and "At Home With Cheryll Gillespie," a weekly one-hour talk show, and is a highly sought after speaker at home and garden, renovation, fashion, and lifestyle shows across North America.

Her fame has spread to the point where her web site, www.cheryll-gillespie.com, enjoys thousands of hits every week, and she has spent much time in Asia designing and decorating luxury homes in Shanghai, China.

Cheryll has followed many of the rules we all hear but seldom adhere to:

- She diversifies so that she has many irons in the fire. She divides her time between television, radio, print media, public appearances, workshops, and design.
- She markets to many publications so that if she loses one it is not a catastrophe. "Syndication seemed obvious. It made sense to me, when I write I write for thirty publications," she says, crediting the availability of e-mail with providing the means to do it efficiently and effectively. "I don't know how people did this twenty years ago. With e-mail you can take a story and send it out to thirty editors at the touch of a button."

- She utilizes what she does in many ways so that she gets the best value from her efforts. "It just didn't make sense [to use the material she had written only once], I wasn't going to do radio show or a newspaper column, if it was only going to sell to one market. Was not going to stay at same level." Her material, she says, is, "Multi-use stuff, each article can get pared down to a ninety-second radio clip. Radio clips make perfect little tip boxes for newspaper to use for fillers or boxed items."
- She constantly markets. "Marketing yourself is a lot of work," she acknowledges, saying she sends out as many as six hundred unsolicited marketing pieces and follows up on the ones that respond.
- She services her clients well and establishes a good relationship with them all. For example, she approached every market that buys her syndicated column individually, one by one. "I'm quick and friendly, say to my clients if you need something quick and specific, ask me. Trying to be their best friend."
- She works hard to keep her material fresh and appealing. "I interview everyone," she laughs. Those people have included such notables as Robin Leach and Hugh Heffner. "People say how do you get these people on a radio show. The answer is simple — I ask! So many other designers have their own show, I feed off them. It's wonderful how everyone shares ideas, networks, helps each other."

Cheryll Gillespie says she is one of those people who believe they can do anything, and who try. If it doesn't work she moves on, but she never closes doors behind her.

- "Believe in what you do."
- Be tenacious: "Until they tell me do not send me any more stuff, quit stalking me, I don't take no for an answer."
- She strives to be her client's best friend. "If you like me you won't change. I think I'm great to work with."

Getting Started or Refocusing

These bits of advice come from a number of writers I look up to, including my hero, Oprah.

- Get quiet: listen to your heart.
- Become aware.
- Answer questions: what would you regret not having done if your life were ending?
- Focus on one passion.
- Brainstorm to overcome obstacles.
- Find encouragement from your peers, put a group together if there isn't one. Find a mentor.
- Face your fears by taking action.
- Exactly what are you afraid of? Ask yourself what will happen if your greatest fear comes true.
- Take one action to move your career forward.
- Open one door, get your butt in gear, and watch what happens.

Chapter Five:
Working From the Home Front

One of the greatest benefits of taking the HBB [home-based business] path in life is the security of knowing you can be self-sufficient while maintaining control over how you spend your day.

Julie V. Watson

There is an individual in my life who has gone through a school of hard knocks that included teenage pregnancy, a failed marriage, and a bout with breast cancer. Through it all she stood firm and did her best. At one point in her life she seemed to have it all, including her own hair salon in an upscale mall in an upscale neighbourhood. As her life went through dramatic changes, she changed her working situation to a home-based business. Instead of the commercial property, with all of its expenses as well as responsibilities of management and being an employer, she stepped back.

Today she operates a home-based business going out to a select clientele to provide hair care services in their own homes. It was a smart move, for it put control of her life into her own hands. With a new relationship, growing children, and a new lifestyle she found the best for her world. Now she can schedule her work around her life. If she wants to head for the cottage she blocks that time off in her appointment book.

It's a similar situation to my own. When I left full-time work in the 1980s I worked from home for a time, then was lured into renting an office downtown. Located in a major hotel, it offered the benefits of high visibility, underground parking, a pool and fitness centre, even discount meals in the staff dining room. But, and it was a big but, it put a huge financial burden on me. I now had rent to pay. Because I was in a traffic flow area I needed to be open during business hours, so a receptionist/secretary came next. Then there were the expenses of posh equipment, insurance, clothes to suit the setting — it was a long list.

To complicate it I had to commute to work; in the winter that drive, although not long, could be very stressful. If I was involved in a big project with a closing deadline I had to spend long hours at the office and away from family. With my husband's medical problems that was often problematical. It was not always easy to transport work home, and when I tried, it always seemed that half of the information I need was back at the office.

Then there is my tendency, especially when I'm into a big project, to take on a persona that combines pack rat and tornado. I literally fill every flat surface, including the floor, with papers, books, research material. All in piles that only I understand. It's my way. Since big projects are never quick projects I constantly presented a cluttered, disorganized image to the world. Our office had big windows opening into a hallway in the hotel. When the blinds and door were closed I felt claustrophobic.

We had also gone through some major lifestyle changes as a couple. After living in the country with horses, dogs, and the freedom of space, we had sold our farm home and moved into an apartment while we decided what to do with the rest of our lives. One day I decided the second bedroom would be a much cheaper office, laid off the secretary (who hadn't worked out anyway), and took the onus off myself to earn that first $2,500 to service the office and staff every month. I could work half the hours and stay at the same income level.

When we purchased our current home I took over what was the family room. Not only was it nice and big, it was hidden away in the basement so my pack rat/clutter bug tendencies were hidden. Working at home has many benefits. If I need to meet with clients I go to them. If my husband is ill I'm right there. I can work the weird hours that suit me best — I love to work early mornings and evenings into late nights, taking the afternoon to get out in the fresh air and walk our dog or run errands. If I play golf for the afternoon I work in the evening. If Jack has evening plans I'll take a few hours off during the day to spend with him. By communicating and cooperating we have developed a lifestyle that is pretty darn nice.

Another change in our lives facilitated my most recent move. I'm out of the basement. While I loved the space, it was a basement with just one small window. The real reason behind this move was that Jack took an early retirement. At the time he retired his health was suffering, so we decided a slight drop in income was a small price to pay to give him time to build a better life.

I was thinking about moving up in the world because the man, as much as I love him, was driving me nuts. He would come to the top of the stairs to ask me things — several times each day. I couldn't hear, so I would have to get up and walk across the basement to the bottom of the stairs to answer. Not a big thing, but I'm a creator. It broke my train of thought. I was actually contemplating replacing my dead laptop so that I could work at the kitchen table when he suggested a move upstairs.

Could have kissed the man. Well, I did, but that's another story. After some discussion we decided I needed the largest of our three bedrooms. The reality was that we needed two guest rooms for only one week a year when his golfing buddies come down from Ontario.

So I finally have the office of my dreams. My desk is right by the window. In the summer we hang a humming bird feeder outside. In the winter chickadees and finches visit daily for a niger seed fix. I can watch the moon rise over the field behind the house. I've been known to sit working in the dark to enjoy the northern lights. Trees, including a glorious old apple, take me through the seasons. These things have fuelled my creativity, and I find my writing has improved immensely. This room has become my favourite place.

Jack built shelves, so I'm surrounded by the books I love, and a fabulous paper holder with fifty-six slots to hold the specialty papers that I use in my work. He built a comfortable place for me to read and do research. He put in a small TV placed on a high shelf that is in my line of sight when working on the computer. We have two desks and two computers. He works alongside me from time to time, as does a woman who is not only my partner in some projects but also a good friend to whom I contract work from time to time.

107

The downstairs office has been converted into a storage room for files, craft market supplies, and overflow books.

Best of all, I'm just steps away from my husband now. We talk more. The sense of isolation is gone. Oh, and the dog is happier. Her little feet used to slip on the hardwood steps going downstairs, so I was constantly having to go and rescue her. She likes having us where she can keep an eye on both of us and not have to worry about missing out on something.

So, what is not to like about being home based? For me, nothing.

Of course, it doesn't work for everyone. Some small businesses thrive in a home office. Others don't. Some folks love to be close to their children. One friend actually hires a housekeeper/nanny yet continues to work at home. It's important, she says, for the children to know she is there, even if not always at their beck and call. Other people find their families too much of a distraction.

We have posted the "Rules of the Inn" by the back door and in the spare bedroom stating in writing that I keep office hours and asking for that to be respected.

For us, the fact that we don't have to go out on a cold winter day when three feet of snow fills the drive is a real plus. We can wait for the snow blower guy to arrive. We enjoy going out for late morning coffee with our friends, or going off to do research together. Jack takes over household chores and dog walking when I have a big project going. I take over when he needs to "crash" for a few days, or golf! I keep flex hours, aiming for forty a week.

Many people start their businesses in their home with the intent of moving to commercial space as soon as financially viable. For others, folks like myself, home is where it's at. And I'm not alone.

Benefits of HBBs

- No commuting time
- Flexible hours
- Availability to family
- Fewer set costs for rent, daycare, etc.
- Tax deductions

Pitfalls of HBBs

- Isolation
- Difficulty budgeting
- Scheduling around family
- No paid benefits
- Danger of working too much

City Dweller to Daylily Queen: Suzanne Johnston

There was a time when we heard of many people choosing to go back to the land in pursuit of a lifestyle out of the rat race. It still happens, often when people pursue their dreams of a new way of life and find that they can incorporate a less stressful, more enjoyable way of earning a living. Such was the case for one British Columbian.

When Suzanne Johnston gave up the city life for the country rhythms of Vancouver Island, British Columbia, she was anxious to try her luck at living off the land. She found her niche in hybrid daylilies.

Today, Kilmalu Farms Daylily Nursery in Cowichan Valley offers daylilies and ornamental grasses to suit every garden and every gardener. So how did this city dweller end up a queen of the daylily set?

"We moved into our new 'house in the country' ten years ago! I can't believe how fast the time has gone. I didn't change careers until a year and a half later, but, yes, it was a successful move. I have never had any regrets since the day I turned in my pager, cell phone, and briefcase for rubber boots, bib overalls, and a pick-up truck to become a 'farmer.'"

Suzanne and her husband, Bob, built their home in a five-acre hay field in Mill Bay, forty-five minutes north of Victoria, in 1993.

"We were married in the house on Boxing Day ... second time for both. We continued commuting to our jobs in Victoria as the weeds grew around us. We had little time to fight it out with Mother Nature over who was going to be in control of the land. By the spring of 1995 it was clear M.N. was winning the battle. Despite the fact that I had never gardened, other than planting a few annuals at my townhouse in Victoria, my solution was to quit my job and start a mail-order nursery."

Changing careers was not new to Suzanne, who had worked as a radio news reporter and a realtor in Victoria and who had dabbled in politics (two terms on Victoria city council and an unsuccessful bid for the provincial legislature in 1991), but the switch from high-profile city life to full-time rural living was "quite dramatic," she says.

"I weeded, took courses, read gardening books and catalogues, researched plants, planted, weeded some more, and planned. By the spring of 1997 I sent out my first mail-order list and began shipping daylilies across Canada. The catalogue business grew and so did our local business. We have now discontinued shipping in order to concentrate on local sales of container-grown plants. I have begun specializing in ornamental grasses along with the daylilies and next year will add lavenders.

"I think the biggest joy has been learning things I knew nothing about, from the plants themselves to fertilizers, soil amendments, and insects to desktop publishing (to produce my own catalogue) and web site design and maintenance (still working on that). I have made lots of mistakes and also learned that it's very hard work and that I'm unlikely to make as much money as I had hoped but I love working outside and

Considering an HBB? Consider This First
- Check bylaws and, if you live in a rental, your lease agreement before going public as an HBB. You don't want any unwelcome fines or problems with landlords.
- Think about traffic flow. Many HBBs operate for years without anyone realizing their existence, simply because they don't receive deliveries or have clients visit their homes. Neighbours are known to complain about the slightest little thing — so think this one through.
- Think insurance, from several angles. First, you should consider a rider on your policy detailing that you are operating an HBB and listing equipment you want covered. Second, you may need liability insurance if you have people coming to your home for anything

related to business. Third, ask your insurance provider about any restrictions. I was recently subjected to having to find another provider because they were concerned about the fact that I was "exporting." I am a writer who focuses on good news–type articles, travel, food, lifestyle — that sort of thing. I only sell one or two pieces outside of Canada each year, yet I was considered a libel risk.
- If you are a parent, especially a parent of young children, there will be interruption. Can you handle that?
- Are you disciplined enough to ignore the housework and other distractions when you need to be working?

being entirely responsible for the success or failure of my own business, from the ground up ... so to speak."

Missing Links, Genealogy Lead to Successful HBB: Sandra Devlin

Ask any East Coast history buff whom they consider the master of genealogy and family histories and they are sure to name Sandra Devlin, who pens "Missing Links," a syndicated column published in a dozen or so Atlantic Canadian newspapers.

Ask Sandra Devlin why she does what she does and she responds, "Because I can. I simply can't imagine any better way to earn a living than to be self-employed, i.e. self-disciplined and responsible only for myself. I think I have the best job in the whole world and that I am doing what I was put on earth to do. There is a lot of job satisfaction, flexible scheduling, and total freedom. Who could ask for more?"

Sandra, of Moncton, New Brunswick, is one of those individuals who follow their own paths, building credits and working up the ladder, and now she has arrived in a place that she really enjoys. It was a path that took thirty years and built her a vast amount of experience.

"Printers' ink got in my veins in 1966. At nineteen and newly married, I walked into the *Fredericton Daily Gleaner* one day looking for a job and was hired on the spot to man a classified advertising desk. I became immediately addicted to the environment of immediacy, proximity to news-makers, and the hectic pace of daily deadlines. A year later, in Guelph, Ontario, I was hired at the *Daily Mercury* where I worked in advertising and circulation before getting my first break into the newsroom.

"In 1978, by then a mother of two small children and living in New Glasgow, N.S. (yes, I am a gypsy), I began working part-time as a weekend family page editor, court reporter, and community correspondent for the *Evening News*, owned by the Thomson Newspaper chain. When both of my children were in school, I joined its news staff as a full-time reporter/photographer. A series of promotions and transfers with Thomson took me (by then a single parent) to Truro, N.S., twice and Kirkland Lake, Ontario."

She won several internal writing competitions and was runner-up in the first-ever national competition for a Thomson Fellowship. After filling the post of managing editor for a number of years, she made a career choice to switch to education. For three years she was the journalism instructor at Holland College in Charlottetown, where she co-authored a revamped curriculum. She also launched a weekly opinion column, which is still running nearly ten years later.

"In 1996 I was again ready for a career change and decided to pursue a long-held ambition to become a full-time freelance journalist. The advent of the Internet made the dream possible. As a cornerstone of my writing business, I launched 'Missing Links,' a weekly, self-syndicated newspaper column specializing in genealogy and family history (a personal passion)."

In May 2002, her column was awarded first place in a prestigious competition sponsored by the International Society of Family History Writers and Editors. She captured two more major awards that spring: winning the first-ever Science Communications award jointly sponsored by Atlantic Provinces Council of the Sciences and Canpolar East Inc. and placing second in the internal newsletter category in a national competition sponsored by the Health Care Public Relations Association. In 1999, she was awarded first place in the annual writers' competition sponsored by the Council of Genealogy Columnists, Inc.

"I think the biggest challenge I have had to face as a freelancer is learning to say 'no.' In the fledgling days of Devlin Ink, when I was getting established and earning a reliable reputation in the new-to-me world of magazine publication and public relations firms, I accepted every assignment with glee. I also accepted every opportunity to speak at genealogical or historical functions in an effort to firmly entrench my syndicated column.

"Eventually, however, I had to convince myself that it was 'okay' to decline work when I became swamped. I had to learn to have confidence that 'work' would continue to come in on a regular basis, even if I turned down the occasional assignment. I have finally found a comfort zone, where I now have pretty much a normal work week, instead of sixty to eighty [hours] per week that I was trying to maintain for a while."

While having her work recognized by peers and nominated for awards is definitely among her proudest moments, she says she is first and foremost a mother and doting grandmother of seven, soon to be nine. "Besides genealogy, I enjoy flower gardening, Scrabble, golf and contract bridge," she says — oh, and when she has time, she plans to write a book or books.

"In a home office, it is especially important to act like a working person," says Sandra Devlin. "'Go to work' every day — on time. Structure your work day strictly, with measured breaks and meal times away from your office. Promote, promote, promote yourself and your skills at every opportunity. To be treated as a working professional, you 'must' act like one and consider yourself to be one."

You and the Tax Man

My financial planner once sent out a notice that began, "The bad new is, there's nothing new that will help cut your tax bill! The good news is, there are already plenty of often underused ways to keep more of what you have earned." I consider my financial planner, Dianne Murphy of Vista Financial Centre Inc., in Charlottetown, to be one of the most important assets we have. We consult her and our accountant before making any changes in our financial situation, including investing, withdrawing money, major purchases, etc. We have saved ourselves many dollars and headaches because we got sound advice from experts. I'm no expert, but I seek help from those who are, and I do have a few bits of advice for the self-employed:

- Keep all receipts in a special file. Not just receipts you think you can deduct, but all receipts. I have two files for receipts: one for business, one for household. If I ever get audited I will have proof that I did not claim every tank of gas, every hotel, or every light bulb, proving that those I did claim are legitimate.
- If you freelance or do consulting work keep a daily log where you record comings and goings, meetings, etc. — the reason behind the deduction. I, for example, do a lot of travel associated with my work. Should there be a question about why I am claiming certain deductions, my log (actually an appointment book where I detail where I go, why, mileage, expenses, etc.) is my evidence that supports my claim. It also helps at tax time when your accountant says, "And why is this expense in here?" You can just refer to your daily log and answer. These records are filed with my income tax receipts each year.
- Get the help of experts. None of us is good at all things. We all have our areas of expertise and things that we are, frankly, bad at. If bookkeeping, taxes, and such are one of the areas where you are not as proficient as you should be, get a professional to help. I had a member of my women in business group come in, set up a spreadsheet program on my computer, and teach me how to use it. I have my taxes done by an accountant, taking these spreadsheets in with my taxes. Much less expensive than taking in a box of receipts for an accountant to sort out. We also never make major decisions regarding money without discussing them with my financial planner and/or my accountant. Over the years, getting their help has saved us thousands of dollars and helped me establish myself with a credit rating.
- Find out what is tax-deductible. If you have a dedicated space for working, the costs can be allocated based on square footage. You can also deduct a portion of utility bills, insurance, maintenance costs, mortgage payments, property taxes, and cleaning costs. As well, all supplies and expenses directly related to your business are 100 percent deductible. Sit down with your tax preparer and discuss what is deductible, when you should make major purchases, and what things affect your taxes.

Marketing and Technology Home Biz Foundation: Tracey Allen

Tracey Allen has a passion for a marketing and technology that translated into a business known as T. Allen & Associates, Inc., based in Charlottetown, Prince Edward Island. With a background in internet training for businesses, a business degree, and a little nudge from a friend in January 1999, Tracey took the leap from executive director of an industry association to starting her own business.

At first Tracey started out with a home-based office in her basement, then moved after the first year to a downtown office location where she stayed for two years before moving back again to a home-based business, but this time in an upstairs office with lots of light and warmth. She will tell you, "For some people and businesses it just makes more sense to have a home office. For me it was all the going back and forth, since I kept two computers, I'd be constantly going from home to office and back again. I discovered that my clients didn't want to visit my location, just salespeople. Being home was also a way to increase my bottom line — which was a nice bonus.

"How do I make $$$ — I've learned to adapt my skills to the client's needs, within my abilities. I'm a professional business writer for fun and a little extra cash in down times while I also use this skill in creating marketing plans, web site updates, press releases for my marketing clients."

Advice from Tracey Allen based on experience:

- I was fortunate to find a mentor to help with consulting in the first year. Use the local associations to assist you to find a mentor. Sometimes a few words of wisdom from someone who has been down that road are all you need to get you over a hump!
- Proposal writing is a lot of work — so pick the proposals you want to write wisely. Look at the competition, your skills, and people who you will be working with on the project then decide if it is worth the time and investment to write a proposal for that project.

- Keep a close eye on your expenses — they can get out of hand quickly. With this in mind, always plan your purchases, and be sure to set up a line of credit to bridge the time from invoicing to payment so you aren't left short to pay your own business bills.
- Networking is a must for home-based businesses — get out into the community and let people know what it is that you do.

Contracting Out

As an HBB operator I know the value of contracting work out when you can't handle it all. I happen to be fairly good at drumming up work, but I sometimes get in a bind when several contracts come in at the same time. One of the challenges I, and dozens of other small businesses, face is the need for differing areas of expertise.

This week I may need a proofreader. Next it's a graphic designer. Then someone to transcribe tapes, or type in a few dozen recipes. Perhaps I need a photographer and food stylist, or a writer, or someone to stuff envelopes, or build a database. Not only would finding an employee with all of these skills be very difficult, I don't want to be responsible for maintaining a payroll and all of the other responsibilities that come with employees.

The answer is, of course, to contract the work out to individuals who have the skill set that I need for that particular job. Contract workers are often fellow freelancers I may hire to help me fulfill a contract one month, then weeks down the road, they may in turn hire me for the same reason.

Tips for contracting out work:

- You are hiring them to do a specific job, so don't hesitate to ask for references and a resume. You need to know that they can not only do the work you need done, but do it according to your direction, on time.
- Draw up a description of work required, then ask for several quotes or bids on the job.

- Make sure that they have the tools required to do the job. For example, if you need computer work done make sure they have the same or compatible software.
- Make sure you are ready for them to start the project on the day chosen. Detail on paper what is required, by when. Put check points in to ensure that work is progressing as it should.
- Once you have discussed the work to be done and hammered out the details (such as where the work will be done, when, and how) draw up a letter of agreement or a contract. If you want one individual, and no one else, to do the work then specify that along with other details. Some might subcontract, so protect yourself against that.
- Payment for work done should be upon receipt of an invoice. Depending on the job, the length of time, etc., you may pay several instalments, but always on receipt of an invoice. If the individual charges GST and a provincial sales tax, they should be included on that invoice.
- Check with your accountant or tax preparer to ensure that you are handling payment properly. You don't want to do it wrong and find there are tax implications down the road. It is best to arrange payment based on an hourly rate or for completion of specific jobs or levels of work done. Using a flat rate or regularly paid fee (say $200 a week for 10 weeks) may trigger queries from Revenue Canada.

Remember these individuals are contracted to do one short-term assignment for you. You are not hiring them. Instead you are purchasing a service from them. Anything that you ask them to do outside of the specific job described in your agreement can be billed as extra work.

Worthy of Note:

- One thing I admire is a person who wants something and finds a way to make it happen. Such is the case with my friend

Debbie Gamble Arsenault of Alexandra, Prince Edward Island. Debbie has, at last count, 863 model horses. She belongs to a national group of model horse enthusiasts and participates in international "events." Now this is a rather expensive hobby at times — just for starters, many of these model horses quickly become collectibles. Debbie is not from a family with discretionary income so she began making tiny miniature saddles, halters, bridles, blankets — all manner of things, which she sold mail order to fund her hobby.

- Michelle Grant, a Calgary artist and also a model horse collector, takes her love for things equine to a high level with her art. Her pencil drawings, watercolours, and acrylic paintings realistically capture the true essence of her favourite subjects. One of the highlights of her career came when the Royal Canadian Mint selected her design to decorate the 2002 Calgary Stampede commemorative coin. After more than fifteen years working full-time she is established as one of Canada's best western artists.

- When Jean Fletcher of Last Mountain Lake Apiaries in Regina, Saskatchewan, realized that they had a surplus of beeswax on hand, she began to look for ways to use it. "We just never made use of the beeswax from our own honey house," she explains. They began making candles: "So much better for you, they purify the air and destroy dust mites." But Jean wanted something different that built on the benefits of this natural ingredient. She began experimenting with her own recipes and was soon marketing Jean's Skin Cream and a product for lip care. The face, hand, and body cream, which they have been marketing for six or seven years now, has a variety of uses ranging from bum care for newborns to rash treatment for adults. Today Jean and her retired husband market their products, which include honey and honey mustard from the apiary, through the farmers' market and mail order. She is involved in new product development and says the ongoing testing for them is one of the things that have held up development of a web site, something she intends to rectify in the near future.

"Let's Meet": Arrange Meetings to Your Advantage

Setting up meetings with clients can be a challenge for the home business operator. Not every HBB is set up to have people come into the home, nor do they have the needed insurance, and in many cases the home does not present the professional image that we want to leave with our clients. As well, it is wise to meet a first-time client, or anyone who makes you uncomfortable (or may be confrontational), away from your home. Unless you have a separate office that is conducive to client meetings, want the client to see your operation, and have a location that is convenient for potential clients, you have to look at other options:

- First and foremost, offer to go to your client. Not only does that take you off the hook, it gives you a chance to check them out. Don't hesitate to pick up brochures or take notes about them while waiting and during meetings. Knowledge is power.
- Check out sources of free or inexpensive meeting or conference rooms. This may be an advantage of membership in a business organization such as the Chamber of Commerce. Don't forget the Small Business Departments at government offices. Quite often they will put a space at your disposal by prior arrangement at no charge. This will not only provide the amenities, but it will also legitimize your business in the eyes of the client. Important for new businesses.
- Restaurants and hotels are also a good choice, but watch for the pitfalls:

    - Check out the location — does it reflect the image you want to portray? Do they have a table that is private enough, and quiet enough, for business discussion?
    - Can you afford it? Remember, if you do the inviting, you had better be prepared to pick up the tab, and you have no control over what clients or potential clients might order! Do they have a liquor license — wine and alcohol can be expensive! If you don't want

to spring for a meal invite the client for coffee mid-morning or mid-afternoon.

- Will the establishment mind if you linger? You can't discuss business, review papers, make presentations, or sign contracts while eating, so this will be an extended visit.
- Do they charge extra for private dining or meeting rooms? These can work wonderfully well and impress, but the cost can be substantial.
- If you find a location that works for you, and that you may use again, tip well. Keep the staff happy and you will have a much better experience.

- Image is important. One of the benefits of a home-based business has to be the saving on clothes. No longer do we have to maintain a special wardrobe for work. However, it is important to dress and act in keeping with both the surroundings of your meeting venue and the client you are dealing with. In a business setting, put yourself on an even status with the others around the table.
- Be prepared. Spend a bit of time looking into meeting room options: libraries, community centres, government offices, association boardrooms, offices, and even apartment buildings. Also check into conference rooms or boardrooms at nearby businesses. You can often arrange to use a room at little or no charge.
- Lastly, prepare your prattle. Instead of saying, "I'll try to find somewhere to meet," say "Let me just check and make sure the meeting room is open and I'll get right back to you."

Home-based Chip Factory: Dorece MacMillan

Potato chips are a natural everywhere in the country, and perhaps nowhere is more appropriate than the province known as "Spud Island." Dorece MacMillan, owner/operator of Prince Edward Island Specialty Chip Company, took her business concept an extra mile by developing unique packaging and uniquely Canadian maple and lobster flavours.

When Dorece had the idea for her business she took a slow approach to development. "I come from a family that has been in business for years, so I decided to try a couple of bags of chips in my sister's shop in the Cavendish Shopping Centre (a popular tourist stop). I loaded the three kids in van and took one dozen out. We put them in an area close to the cash and I went back to the van for the next box. By the time I got back they were gone. I knew right there and then that I had a winner."

The tourist season was almost over, but the chips were still selling as fast as she could stock them. The following spring Dorece went personally to eight different places in the tourist area, starting with regular flavour chips.

"Everyone I approached put them in their store. They sold really well."

She did all deliveries, with three kids in the van at all times. She laughs that she would bribe them with the promise of candy if they were "really good, didn't fight, and didn't complain." The two oldest helped with stocking shelves. And a daughter and friends packaged the chips in their living room.

At the end of that season she looked at how well sales had gone in those outlets and knew it was going to succeed. Shortly afterwards, Prince Edward Island Business Development arranged the first Prince Edward Island trade show for food products. She participated and had to bring in a couple of friends to help write up orders.

"We got about sixty brand new accounts all over the Island."

The increased business meant she had to redesign her packaging to meet government standards and hire sales/delivery help as well as more chip baggers. The increased business also meant that she turned the ground floor of her two-storey home into a chip packaging area.

She laughs about it now, saying the kids had couches and chairs in their bedroom. The dining room became the receiving area, the living room was assembly and packaging, and the TV room served as holding for delivery.

"That's how we operated the first year. We did fairly well and the next summer developed lobster flavour chips."

She was also able to acquire use of a building on her property, which has now been converted for production and warehousing. "We are able to conduct the business out of that, so had our home back."

Two seasons later she developed maple chips, a flavour reminiscent of a maple-roasted nut.

P.E.I. Specialty Chips have proven very popular in the United States, and Dorece now has a number of off-Island accounts.

She doesn't cook the chips herself but rather has agreements that protect her product, preventing the processors from making them for anyone else. They are delivered to her in cello bags as special orders. It was difficult to find someone who would take her seriously and make the chips for her. Especially the lobster flavour, as she says no one wanted to take a chance on a very small business.

She isn't sure whether people buy her chips for the flavours or the packaging, authentic P.E.I. Potato bags, which she developed herself.

"I'm my own marketing agent, lawyer, do everything myself," except, she laughs, "I have the brains not to be my own bookkeeper. One night I felt like chucking the towel in because I couldn't get my first design to meet federal regulations and couldn't think of a way to make it work. There seemed to be no other way around the red tape that would display the product properly. I went to bed and said a prayer. When I woke up in the a.m. it was in my mind. Ran my idea by the labelling inspector and he said, 'Great idea.'"

Dorece MacMillan advises people to know their strengths and weaknesses, saying, "If you are not good at marketing and selling at a trade show, it's OK you don't have to be. You have other talents. Get someone to do for you who is able to do it well and properly."

And, she says, "Remember the old cliché, enthusiasm is contagious. It's our family's oldest saying, but is vital. If you, or the person marketing for you, are not enthusiastic about your product forget it. It's an old cliché but it's so true and very powerful. If you don't believe, if you can't be enthusiastic, delay launching until you are."

The most difficult part of development was getting someone to take her seriously. "It was very hard. I don't know if it was because I'm a woman or what."

Perhaps it was her enthusiasm that swung things around. "I had tried other things, but this one, I was really enthused about and knew it was it. The others didn't touch me the way this did."

Go Get Organized: Tami Reilly

Six years ago, British Columbian Tami Reilly couldn't keep her head above her paperwork. She was a small business owner with a growing client base and growing client paperwork! Often she had to make a decision forced by time: tidy up or call a client? "Naturally the client came first. Soon, however, papers got lost, bills were missed, and invoicing was delayed. Not a smart way to grow a business," she says on her website, www.gogetorganized.com.

Tami tried many ways to get organized, but within a few weeks she'd be back in the same frustrating situation. Part-time administration people were interviewed, hired, trained, but then eventually moved on or were not suitable. Soon she'd be back to square one, minus a lot of time and money. Finally she decided to do something about it.

As a small business owner, she dreamed of what her ideal office would look like, and how it would make her business easier to run and more successful. She knew what she needed was a tidy workspace with everything easily accessible and easily put away. If she had a crazy week it would be okay because in her ideal office, someone would come in weekly and make it right again. Someone at the right price, with strong management skills, who understood the challenges of a small business.

Was she just daydreaming, or could it really be possible? It was, she decided, and she set to work. The result was organization and a new business. The GoSystem™ allows business owners to delegate the paperwork and sales support in order to have more time to focus on growing their business. Six years and hundreds of clients later, GO's products and services continue to be the answer for the growing pains of many a business owner, including Tami!

In addition to personally helping business owners get organized, she has now produced a CD, including her time-saving techniques and methods for organizing, which clients can apply in their office.

"I tell them everything they need to know to set up a Get Organized day for their company, and on that day, I talk them through the steps as they and their helper organize, so they'll always know exactly what to do and when to do it."

Chapter Six:
Senior Status: The Golden Era

Ask any successful entrepreneur and they'll tell you — it's all about attitude! That doesn't mean you have to strut your stuff for all to see. It's not even about determination. It simply means you have to have the right mindset to succeed.

Julie V. Watson

Senior status is a confusing term these days. Retailers anxious to attract business often offer "senior discounts" to anyone over fifty-five. Early retirement packages often allow people to start collecting a private pension even earlier. Even Canada Pension can be accessed at age sixty.

Yet, with our improved health, lifestyles, and satisfying careers, most individuals feel they are just reaching their prime at these ages. Joints may creak a little more, but general health and fitness are not much different from when we were forty. Frankly, even though many can retire, and are eager for change, they are not ready to stop working and assume the traditional laid-back retirement role of days past.

Aside from the obvious good health, what most retirees want comes down to independence, change, and freedom to choose. Remaining independent is a major priority for most Canadians, and so is the opportunity to enjoy things that have been put off until the stage of life often described as the golden years.

The problem for many of us is that our retirement income is not sufficient to maintain the lifestyle we dream of, the adventures we crave, or even the comforts we envisioned. In fact, according to statistics released recently, things have not improved for senior women in more than thirty years.

According to the Coalition of Provincial & Territorial Advisory Councils on the Status of Women, in 1970, half of all senior women lived in poverty. Today, half of all senior women still live in poverty.

Add to that the fact that many women were the sole support for their families, and/or did not have the privilege of pension plans and other benefits, and you have a situation that leaves many, many senior women needing to work to make ends meet. Since it becomes increasingly difficult to find employment that pays a good wage and is physically possible as we age, many women turn to self-employment.

Many of us also want the satisfaction and sense of worth that comes with our work. We are used to working, to achieving, to providing, and to having the social interaction that comes with working. And then there is the fact that, as one eighty-six-year-old put it, we "just feel too darn young to quit being productive and lounge about."

Although we hear a lot about fifty-five being the age of freedom, the reality is that rising costs, crumbling financial resources, and insurance with so many exceptions it is basically worthless are in fact forcing to many individuals to continue to be concerned about earning money.

A 2002 Statistics Canada Survey showed that nearly a third of middle-aged Canadians felt they hadn't set aside enough money to maintain their standard of living when they retire. That percentage would surely increase if limited to women. Many women do not have private pension coverage, and many self-employed women don't pay into Canada Pension. As well, many women do not own their home and have lower levels of income.

Factors that influence the "continue earning" way of thinking include:

- Fear of not being independent and in charge.
- The feeling that they must continue to accumulate money just in case they live into their nineties.
- More user fees being applied to everything from health care to banking.

- Costs of everything from car insurance to food increasing at an alarming rate.
- Pensions not keeping up with real inflation.
- Investments such as RRSPs having taken a hit that many feel they will never recover from.
- Insurance failing to offer the protection anticipated, increasingly too costly or unavailable.
- Savings often being eaten up caring for spouses or parents.

So what are seniors getting up to? You will be surprised at the diversity! During a visit to Edmonton we met a couple of grand ladies who should be role models for us all.

Agent Going for Forty Years in Show Biz: Maureen Saumer

My first contact with Maureen Saumer came via the telephone. My sister-in-law met this woman, whom she called a charmer, got her number, and insisted I talk to her for my book. She answered after several rings and immediately apologized for her husky voice, explaining that after having a lung removed, and three strokes, "they" insisted she keep having these checkups and tests done.

"One damaged my throat, made my voice a bit husky. I used to sing and dance all the time," she chuckled, "my voice wasn't a bit husky then. Tried to dance the other day, lost my balance and nearly fell on my nose!"

Within minutes I learned that she came to Canada from England as a war bride, after marrying a Canadian combat World War II fighter pilot. Her new mother-in-law was shocked that she didn't like tea, and that she had once been a hostess at what is now the Holiday Inn but "was a Red Cap then." After just a few minutes I knew I had to meet the feisty woman on the other end of the phone.

Getting together with this seventy-six-year-old agent for performing artists proved a challenge. She keeps a schedule that would defeat many people thirty years her junior.

"My week's going to be very busy," she explained. "I've got reflexology, I'm taking shocks for carpal tunnel. Then tomorrow we're going to the Klondike 'do,' an annual Edmonton event nominating the Klondike Kate and Town Crier for Klondike days."

It's an important affair for Maureen, who was the main booking agent for "Klondike" for several years. Oh, and she was meeting with a man from the airbase about some entertainment.

Finally a day was set. They would drive to the part of the city where I was staying to save me having to travel.

Seated in Kelsey's Restaurant, in North Edmonton, Maureen, her beloved husband, Paul, my son, John, and I began a chat that proved to be a most enjoyable interview. Maureen, who still sports a hint of merry England in her raspy voice, told us the tale of her arrival in Edmonton to work in nightclubs, where she got her start in a business now known as Guild Hall Productions.

"One day, Hank DiMarco, a musician working for Wilber Wright in Jasper Park Lodge, asked if I would like to get into business. I said I know nothing. He said not true, he'd watched me working with entertainers and was impressed by how I talked to them, handled them.

"I did a little entertaining — was good at drama and poetry — very good at that, wasn't I, Paul. I was a dancer, could jitterbug, couldn't I, Paul." The patient and loving Paul smiles and nods his head. "I was always singing opera. My wish was to become a famous opera star and all I did was become a booking agent for the stars," she chortled.

She began representing performers, hired first as a subagent; after six months, her mentor, she said, "took me to the Union. That's how you do it, train first."

She gets 12 percent commission per show booked. Now in her thirty-seventh year as an agent, she says she is determined to continue even though the downturn in the economy is making it tougher

"I'm still doing it because I enjoy it. Would like to make forty years in the business before I think about retiring."

One of three leading agents in Edmonton, and the longest in the business, she has over one thousand acts in her file. "I don't have to go out now but when I first started I would have to go around to the taverns and clubs to find clients to represent."

Now they hear about her and bring their credentials. She works from home. "I did have an office, but it got too expensive paying rent, promotion, and all of those things. It's hard going today to be a booking agent."

When she required new artists Maureen would place an ad in the paper. "That paid off." She belongs to Alberta Culture, "a big association here you have to belong to and my artists are in the book, the Arts Touring Alliance of Alberta, a Directory of Touring Artists."

She represents a number of performers ranging from music groups to puppet troups, magicians, and event choirs. She books puppet theatre, murder mysteries, and belly dancers.

Through the course of her career she met such stars as Gracie Field, Nana Muskori, and Ann Murray, and brought Sherri Lewis, Dela Reese, and the first belly dancer to Edmonton.

"I do it the old way," she says, "write out by hand and then go and get photocopied. Computers scare me even though my daughter is a computer programmer with clients all over the world. Paul does all of the typing — with two fingers."

We should all find the sheer enjoyment in life that these two zany Edmontonians (Maureen the agent and Paul the support team) have, in spite of Maureen's illness.

When I asked Maureen if she has any advice to pass along she handed me a sheet of paper titled "The Difference between Winners and Losers." On it was written:

- A winner works harder than a loser and has more time; A loser is always "too busy" to do what is necessary.
- A winner goes through a problem; A loser goes around it, and never gets past it.
- A winner says, "I'm good, but not as good as I ought to be"; A loser says, "I'm not as bad as a lot of other people."

Opportunity Knocks

An explosion of new technological products designed to help seniors and people with disabilities maintain independence has burst onto the market. These products, and services as well, not only help seniors stay in their own homes longer, but also make it easier to maintain a small business.

They represent an opportunity to develop products and services for this ever-growing market. After all, who better to understand the needs of seniors than seniors themselves?

Consider this: understanding high-tech, from digital cameras and complicated software to initiating newbies to computers, the world of e-mail, web searching, and writing letters on the computer, is tough for all ages, especially some seniors, who have never been exposed to such things before.

Personalized one-on-one, explanations of how to use such and such, setting up equipment like televisions and DVD players — all of these present opportunities to provide services for people. Then there are services like shopping for those who can't or don't want to go themselves, even transporting people to the doctor or out for the day.

When starting to research information on existing products, services, and challenges faced by seniors seeking to retain their independence, one place to contact is the Canadian Mortgage and Housing Corporation, at 1-800-668-2642 or www.cmhc.ca. They can get you started with information about suggested renovations to the home, which is one change seniors may require.

Spreading the Christian Word: Verna Becker

Edmonton's Verna and Clarence Becker met when they were missionaries working on the Ivory Coast in West Africa. Throughout their married life, religion and missionary work, at home and abroad, has directed their life. A number of years ago Clarence was working half time, travelling with a mission selling Christian literature to bookstores.

"He came home one day when I was making arrangements for a tour through British Columbia. Three or four of the bookstores I called to set up sales appointments had closed due to finances.

"I said to Clarence, 'I'm depressed, here we are driving all this way from Edmonton, and all these area bookstores are closing down. How are we going to meet the needs of the people?'"

The couple are great believers in the importance of making more good reading material available, "books that build up instead of bringing down." At about the same time they learned about New Life Distribution and Marketing Co. Ltd., in Sherwood Park, Alberta.

"We were told you have to meet this couple and we did."

Glenna and Eugene Barton had founded the "New Life" business/ministry in 1984 to provide Christian literature through a network of distributors. Those distributors sell the books by many means: in mall displays, at retreats and conventions, by racking (arranging with a retail outlet to set up a rack of books for a shared profit), to libraries, through home parties, and so on. They shared their vision to penetrate clean across Canada with good moral-building literature, something that immediately appealed to the Beckers.

"We started working with people, placing racks, distributing, and we developed camp work," says Verna, explaining that they set up a table to sell books at family camps held by various churches or organizations.

"That has been very profitable. We are preparing for three camps this summer. It's fun, they accept us as part of the staff, so that to us it's a holiday. They look after us, make our meals."

She says this after-retirement business has been very meaningful for them. "We feel we are being ministered to in every part of life."

Their move into distribution of New Life material was in some ways a leap of faith. "My husband worked very hard and we didn't have any finances. The night we met Eugene and Glenna Barton, we were coming home when Clarence said we've got books, and we've got a business, but we'll never make much money with the inventory we have. We need to buy more."

Verna had $400 that had been tucked away since her mother had passed away.

131

"I always wanted to invest in something that would have an ongoing ministry. That was our first investment and it's been a tremendous ministry and investment."

The business was not a fast money builder because of the need to have inventory.

"Clarence was still working when we invested that $400 from mother and we reinvested money back into business until it was established. Each book touches people's lives. I used to count books and multiply and think *wow!* I've touched all of those lives. It ended up being a fantastic business. Our son does the computer work. When I started I did inventory, orders, invoice everything by hand. All calculated in my head. Man, he said, you have got to use a calculator. Didn't trust them then," she laughed. "I would do it and add up in my head to make sure it was right."

Even though they are at a stage in life when most people settle back to bask in retirement, Verna and Clarence are very active entrepreneurs, a natural thing for people who have been involved in business all of their lives.

"This has given us fulfilment. I enjoyed some of the other businesses but with this we are selling things that affect people."

Their product line includes devotional books, novels and non-fiction, kids' books, inspirational videos, cassettes, giftware and stationery, and of course bibles. They also look for other distributors to work with them and, just to keep life interesting, are involved in several other endeavours. Verna was quick to demonstrate a "Chi machine," which she markets. Clarence makes frames for art and religious sayings.

"If anyone had told me we would have such a fulfilling retirement I wouldn't have believed them."

"Always have goals, something to stretch for. As seniors it's very important that we keep on learning," says Verna Becker, stressing that it is important for seniors to keep on being interested in something, to keep moving ahead. "If we allow our minds to become stagnant, then they will stop working. I live on the phone. Built business on the phone, encouraging, advising, organizing." And, she says, "If you are going to do this in your eightieth year, we realize it is very important to keep our health — very vital, very important."

Wrist Rat: Sylvia Ross

Some time ago I received a rodent as a gift. A friend knew I was having a problem with sore wrists, presumably caused by working so many hours at the computer, so she sent me a Wrist Rat. Now, I don't like rodents or creepy crawlies or slithery things, but I did grow attached to my Wrist Rat. He was kind of soft, plush, and just right for providing a comfortable prop for my arm while I worked my mouse. The story of its development and success is an excellent model for others to follow, for its creator analyzed what was needed, worked to develop a good product, sought help with business start-up, protected her investment, and approached it all with a determination to retain the lifestyle she wanted.

Wrist Rat was developed by Sylvia Ross of North Bay, Ontario, when her sister was experiencing computer mouse–related wrist discomfort. She went shopping, but all of the wrist supports she found were uncomfortable.

"To the drawing board as they say ... I wanted something that would be adjustable and comfortable at the same time. The type of stuffing was critical since it could not cause any static build-up in a computer environment. Oats seemed to be ideal! I tried out other stuffing and realized that with foam, static could be a problem. My theory was that if the cushion retained its shape, then a user could leave the mouse to use the keyboard and then return to the mouse with the cushioned support ... just the way it was left ... contoured in a comfortable fit for the wrist."

The first prototype was too long, the next was too fat, then came one that was too short! By trial and error Sylvia reached the correct size. The comfortable cushion aligns the arm and hand by supporting the wrist while mousing, thus ensuring less stress on the nerve within the carpal tunnel.

"Just for fun I added some whiskers ... it resembled something like a mole! When eyes, nose, ears, and tail were added it took on a rat-like appearance and it wasn't long before the 'Wrist Rat' got 'er name!"

She tested the Wrist Rat using her sister and friends.

"But having an idea, and developing a product were one thing ... but where do you go with an idea?" she wondered. This was an area where she had no expertise.

"In 1995 I opted for an early retirement from Transport Canada, ending a career of almost twenty-nine years. My former position as a Manager of Resources in the federal government did not equip me with the skills for a successful entrepreneurial venture. I applied for an Entrepreneur Training Program through Nipissing East Community Opportunities. I presented my business idea, a sampling of my product ... and I was accepted into a forty-week training program."

The training program started with the basics of developing a business plan and touched on many areas, including accounting, marketing, advertising, time management, sales, and motivation. This was an ideal forum to learn from others who were also starting out in various business endeavours. One area that she says was of the most help was developing confidence in the product or service you were intending to market.

With completion of the training, it has been off to the "rat races"! The legwork starting out included securing the licence for the business. Of course, this only came after the business name of The Rat Works was chosen. Although the rodents are small, a provincial permit for the stuffing was required (as evidenced by the label on each Wrist Rat), approval for the labelling of the outer covering was obtained from the federal government, a PST permit was acquired, an application for an Industrial Design was submitted, a logo was designed, packaging and labels were manufactured, and advertising materials were obtained. The classroom training was completed in November 1996; however, it was not until March 1997 that the first Wrist Rat was packaged and sold.

The Rat Works contracted with G&P Consulting for the distribution, and it was in March that the first commercial account was secured. Sylvia says that it was a thrill to see her product on the shelves of a local office supply store. Several commercial outlets now retail Wrist Rats.

An application to the Canadian Intellectual Property Office resulted in the Wrist Rat being accepted as an Industrial Design. The Rat Works is hoping to negotiate a license for manufacturing. In the meantime, even though Sylvia considers herself to be a retiree, she did the manufacturing herself with a first production run of two thousand.

Soon orders were flowing in from across Canada and beyond, many resulting from a small item about her in *Good Times* magazine.

As a grandmother in her fifties, Sylvia says she can recommend starting out in a home-based business as an option for persons wishing to become involved in business with a limited investment. She has a word of caution, however: no matter how small you may want to keep it, sometimes a business can grow beyond your expectations.

And does she mind being referred to as "The Rat Lady"? She says, "Not at all, it's great advertising! Just remember these Rats make great pets, they are obedient, in that they stay just where they are left and don't need to be fed or walked. And to keep your pet from straying, there is a place for ID right on 'er label."

"My rats have really travelled!" says this retiree who is a fountain of knowledge and generous with her advice for other retirees starting a small business.

"I would suggest contacting Human Resource Canada to see if they are running any courses which are geared to establishing small businesses. Sometimes they sponsor workshops that are ideal for anyone interested in starting a small business," she says. "Of course, it is necessary to do lots of homework and research prior to making any financial investment — and a business plan is an absolute necessity.

"Sometimes funding is available for small business start-up ... that is a grant and not a loan. This is usually funded jointly through federal, provincial, and municipal programs. During periods of high unemployment programs are established to assist business with start-up costs if they have sound business ideas, a good business plan, and there is potential for future employment. This avenue is worth exploring."

When she started The Rat Works she was able to secure a grant, which allowed her to have a professional design brochures and paid for printing of brochures and business cards, etc., as well as a banner for use at trade shows.

"I would suggest a good book is an excellent investment — such as *The Complete Canadian Small Business Guide* (Douglas and Diana Gray) published by McGraw-Hill Ryerson. If someone is going to apply for a Patent or an Industrial Design for a product — then perhaps they should contact Industry Canada for advice prior to offering the product for sale."

She did the paperwork herself to register the Wrist Rat as an Industrial Design. "The staff at the Canadian Intellectual Property Office were a great help. I explained that I was going to do the work myself instead of hiring someone — so they provided me with booklets and forms and lots of tips. My design was registered and now I just have to renew it every five years. And by doing the work myself I saved a bundle for my company."

During a visit to Edmonton I chatted with a gracious lady who supplements her pension by selling goods at a local flea market where she has a regular Sunday table. She makes some crafts, and also shops yard sales and such for items to resell. Larger items are saved up and she has a yard or garage sale, depending on the weather. She needs the money, she said, as her "Old Age" isn't enough. As important, she enjoys her life as a trader and says she meets "grand people" at the market. "We arrive early and have coffee. Then we help each other with the packing up."

Tips for Yard/Garage Sale Success

Yard sales are a grand way to get rid of all the excess stuff, and they can be turned into a microbusiness if you enjoy the buying and selling game. We asked a few folks their secrets of attracting the good crowds with dollars to spend that spell success for your yard sale.

When advertising, or making up posters, use a few of the magic words for yard sale shoppers:

- Collectibles
- Everything must go
- Multiple families
- Moving
- Bargains

Make big, bold signs using these words and use them on sale day.

Be prepared to reduce prices and offer specials such as two-for-one on items that are not moving by mid-point in your sale. Either have signage made or have the materials to make them on hand. Don't rely on being able to tell people; you might be tied up with someone else and lose a sale. As one person put it, "You can unload twice as much stuff if they think they are getting a bargain, and I don't have to lug it back to the basement."

Price everything and be prepared to dicker. For some the haggling is the best part of the day.

Get on your feet and work your customers. It's really tempting to just sit in a chair, cash box at hand, and rake in the money by letting folks bring their purchases to you. Truth is, anyone who has worked trade shows, or who does this type of selling for a living, will tell you contact with people — being friendly, giving them a laugh, or making them feel good — will get you a sale. You can sweeten the deal: drop the price or throw in an extra, extol the virtues of the product and tell them its history or reliability. In other words, you can chat with your customers, create a fun atmosphere, and sell more.

And as for all of those little things, like ornaments, jewellery, and such: don't just chuck them in boxes. Take a hint from the pros again. Get some dark fabric or a tablecloth — you can often get velvet in the remnants bin, or at a yard sale — and display these small items on it. Put them into the category of collectibles.

A Spudly Endeavour: Doreen Wood

Two individuals who really inspired me were Doreen and John Wood of Young's Cove in Kings County, New Brunswick. I was working at an Aquaculture Trade Show in St. Andrew's, New Brunswick, and took a few hours off to attend a craft show held down on the waterfront the same weekend. Lunch was the first order of the day, and I was lured by the sight and smell of fresh-cut spiral potatoes being deep fried by the couple and sold for four dollars per plateful.

Naturally we got to chatting. Turns out Doreen is a retired schoolteacher. John was an operations manager with the power company. The couple wanted something to do that would add to their lives, and to their pocketbooks. John rigged up a gizmo with an electric drill that cut a potato into one big, long spiral, about the thickness of a potato chip. When they get a customer John zaps the spud, Doreen fries it up in the deep fryer, while John handles the money side — takes just a couple of minutes for a plateful of tasty, hot potato chips.

The couple choose the events they want to visit each summer and travel in their truck and fifth-wheel trailer, which they say their little business paid for.

"It's a great way to travel and we get to meet some wonderful people."

"Get to know the products that you work with and your suppliers. We found a specific potato and a certain size were important to us."

Publishing Business on a Bet: Ursula Maxwell-Lewis

When a semi-retired publisher made a bet with Ursula Maxwell-Lewis, of Surrey, British Columbia, it started a chain of events that resulted in the creation of the *Cloverdale Reporter News* and Ursula donning multiple hats as publisher, managing editor, freelance writer, and photographer.

"The *Reporter* was started on a bet with $500 in the bank (which I wanted back as fast as possible!)," Ursula explains. "A semi-retired publisher bet me that I could start (and run) a community newspaper. I bet him that I couldn't. I said I would give it three months — if he helped me with layout.

"Nine months later my twenty-seven-year-old marriage became a thing of the past, so did my finances, and it was sink or swim. Being in my mid-fifties, I decided I'd better increase my circulation in more ways than one!"

She stuck with it rather than seeking employment because, "Like Topsy, the business seems to keep growing — so I keep on going! At my age I'm not entirely sure what else to do. It also means I don't have to punch a clock, worry about strike votes, or do what someone else tells me. I'm a true Aquarian — an impractical dreamer!"

There were many challenges to face along the way: divorce, insecurity ("combined with some hysteria"), insolvency, and "competition from major publications when they realized I wasn't going away."

She says the worst time she had was when she realized the business had grown beyond her capabilities. She desperately needed help and couldn't afford it.

"I felt it was an absolute albatross around my neck, but was too stubborn to quit. Out of the blue an advertising specialist arrived in my office. He knew exactly what I was aiming at, and how to get there. It was a huge relief, and reminded me that if you surround yourself with expertise you might just end up looking pretty good, and win a round or two in the end."

She didn't come into the community newspaper business totally unprepared. She had worked as a journalist in South Africa in the early 1960s. "So, at least I knew a bit — not much — about community newspapers. I certainly had no idea about the inner workings of any business. I also worked in the travel industry as a flight attendant, customer relations correspondent, passenger agent, and other such things before giving in to domesticity."

That domesticity resulted in three "marvellous children and two adorable grandsons."

Working with the motto, "Keeping the Independent Community Spirit Alive," she has grown that $500 investment into the only community newspaper delivered by Canada Post to 42,000 readers in British Columbia's heritage Clover Valley.

She also publishes *Travl'n Times*, is a member of the Travel Media Association of Canada (serving as president of the B.C. chapter from 1997 to 2001), is director and co-sponsor of the very successful Surrey International Writers' Conference (www.siwc.ca), and is director of the Surrey Tourism Advisory Council.

Today, she says, she is looking at retiring so that she can keep on writing and travelling. "In the meantime, I am considering a quarterly travel tab if the advertising support is available. So far it looks promising."

Yeah right, with this schedule retirement is still a long way off, Ursula.

Ursula Maxwell-Lewis suggests that others starting or in business, "Explore the availability of grants, and study how to 'grow your business' effectively. Since the success of my whole project really took me by surprise I did neither and was very unprepared. This caused additional stress — which good planning could probably have eliminated. And don't go into debt. Pay attention to the bottom line. That's what counts. It's all about finance, not romance."

Decadent and Delicious at the Market: Dina Sippley

Walking through the Moncton Farmers' Market I was offered a sample of sugar pie. It was delicious enough to stop me in my tracks — I love good sugar pie. As I dug in my purse for the eight dollars I needed to buy a small pie, Dina Sippley told me they were made with her exclusive recipe.

"A Quebec recipe. If you go to Quebec all restaurants have sugar pie. Mine is special because it's made with real churned butter. You compare with one pound of regular butter and you will never switch back. It has a little buttermilk taste — fait au beurre baratte," she spells.

"For me it's important. I will not tamper with my recipe! People don't know what my

Decadent and delicious sugar pie keeps retiree Dina Shippley busy producing Cuisine "Dina" gourmet treats for the Moncton Farmers' Market in New Brunswick.

sugar pie is like here in Moncton," she says to explain her sampling. "They have to have a chance to try it to know what it's like."

Her passion would guarantee sales, even if her food weren't amazingly delicious. Operating as Cuisine "Dina" she offers up a number of traditional goodies each Saturday, including salmon, chicken, turkey, beef or pork paté, tourtière, chowders, and much, much more.

It was quite a surprise to learn that Dina has not always made her living cooking. Turns out she had worked a sales rep for a door and window manufacturer whose head office is in Quebec. She opened Cuisine "Dina" after she retired.

Worthy of Note

- At the same market Rachel LeBlanc of Memramcooke, New Brunswick, was selling Goose Tongue Greens — four dollars a pound, "only at the market when they're in." Same with Samphire Greens, she explained. It's a little extra money each spring when she gets out to harvest the traditional wild greens found in the marsh areas around the Bay of Fundy.

- An aunt always impressed me with her approach to retirement. She had had a long and successful career in banking, but a combination of things, including a health issue, helped her make the decision to retire early. She just didn't want to devote the energy and time to commutes and a high-pressure job. But she had knowledge and skills that she utilized for several years, working with people who were facing buyouts or had severance packages and retirements options to consider. With this part-time consulting work she was able to adjust to suit her own schedule and lifestyle.

- Visitors from British Columbia told us about a seventy-year-old gal who lives at British Columbia's Gold Coast region and who purchased herself snow cone and popcorn machines. She starts in early June and sells at the beach throughout the summer, at Girl Guide camps, school sport days, church picnics, Lions events, and at the annual parade. The retired teacher is involved with many things in her community and is considered part of the local scene.

When interviewing a WIB for one of the other chapters, she made a comment that is a fitting end for a chapter that focuses on those just waving toodle-oo to middle age.

"Remember, Julie," she said, "when the big topic we discussed was prejudice against women in business? Sure, that's still there. We still have problems of invisibility, even when we're in the same room.

"Now, at sixty-one, I notice that age-ism is creeping in, as common wisdom would have us retired, living off our generous employer pension plans. Lenders and such are a bit uncomfortable dealing with people our age with 'big ideas.' Maybe the Chamber of Commerce should start a 'Women-Who-Don't-Know-When-To-Quit Committee.'"

Maybe she was just being facetious, but what she says has merit. We need to take up this cause through some organization — and by going public.

Chapter Seven:
Artisans, Craftswomen Rock

Never have a group of individuals demonstrated such a varied array of creative skills as those produced by artisans and craft producers. Not only do they create wonderful one-of-a-kind pieces and handcrafted items to be treasured, these women also rule at self-sufficiency, running their own businesses and committing to a lifestyle of their choosing. To make a living as an artisan takes a special kind of spirit, creativity, and dedication.

Julie V. Watson

These are the self-motivators, the women who work in studios or in home workshops. They are creators whose skills range from fabric arts to pottery, from photography to stone carving, from fantasy figures to weaving ... the list is endless.

One of the best places to get a feel for the diverse opportunities and career options open to women in the arts and crafts sector is an exhibition or craft fair. Walk in with the approach that you are looking for inspiration and open your mind to receive. For you are entering a world unto itself.

At the Fair

Craft fairs have a special feeling in the air during the hours before the doors are thrown open for the first surge of eager shoppers. Set-up is a time of hard work tempered by an eager anticipation — a buzz in the air. There is a special camaraderie between vendors preparing their displays. It's part of life for many artisans.

From coast to coast, these events showcase women making money. For some this is a full-time business; for others it's a way to supplement their income, to get extra cash for vacations, kid's college expenses, or Christmas shopping. The fair can, in fact, be an unusual mix of folks, booths ranging from elaborately built set-ups that take hours to assemble to a simple table with a tablecloth from home and a few goods modestly displayed.

The variety of products ranges from woodwork to pottery, from sewn clothing to handwoven tableware, from cookbooks to fudge and antipasto, from toys to collectible treasures.

In fact, the goods for sale at any fair are so varied that it can boggle the mind. The creativity and imagination they demonstrate is wonderful thing to behold. Here you will find a true mix of small businesses. Some are home-based, others are not. Some are true artisans, creating original pieces and works of high value. Others are packagers or assemblers, creating lower end, but just as important, items. Sophisticated to country, fantasy to practical, the marketed goods come in all shapes, sizes, and prices.

You will never have a true perspective of how much this is a business to most vendors until you visit a fair during that set-up time. People lug in cumbersome displays and box after box of handcrafted merchandise. All carefully packed and transported, often from miles away.

Talk is of how the show will be, how shows before were, how they did in other cities or towns, where they are going next. It's a lifestyle. For anyone serious about making their living this way the months of November and December, as well as the summer, mean weekends on the road. Packing up goods to sell, loading in display units, driving miles, unpacking, setting up, then spending one to five days smiling, answering questions, smiling, selling, making change, smiling, packaging, and finally packing up everything that is left and dismantling the booth, ready for the next show. Overnighting in hotels or campers, taking meals on the fly — usually during lulls in business — it's all part of the craft fair business. The scenario I've described is not unusual.

It is also financially uncertain. At the beginning of a fair there is great expectation, but no certainty, about what sales will be.

As one person commented when discussing how she had been doing at various fairs, "It's survival of the fittest. We just keep plugging. Reality is that while you do well at some fairs, you may not do well at all of them. Some are going to be better than others. What I do is look at my end of season totals."

That said, for some people this is a wonderful way to make a living. It gets in your blood, and as tired as you are at the end of a fair, you eagerly anticipate the next one.

Invest in Style, Movin' on Up: Bev Doman

One such individual is Bev Doman. To set the scene, Bev and Terry Doman were sharing a classroom with us at Three Oaks Craft Fair in Summerside. The Domans, from Dartmouth, Nova Scotia, were "on the circuit."

Bev's business, InVEST In Style, produces colourful handmade reversible vests, shirts, sweatshirts, aprons, half aprons, baby books (fabric), scrunchies, and country crafts. Her main focus is the vests, which are unique because they are themed. She has vests for all seasons and for holidays like Christmas, Halloween, and Easter. She also has some with Velcro attachments that can be "designed each day according to your mood." Music notes, bingo jackpots, school days,

Bev Doman's creative flair with the needle takes InVEST In Style that extra step that spells success. The Nova Scotian sewer takes to the craft fair circuit to market her wares.

cooks, country themes, chickens, horses, sunflowers, even the ocean liners that ply the Atlantic are featured in her fabrics.

145

During set-up Bev had very definite ideas of what should go where. This lady had obviously thought things through, observed her customers, and taken a businesslike approach to merchandizing. Between sales she methodically checked stock against her records, perhaps to see what to replenish. Later, she pinned projects together, getting ready for the machine or hand sewing. There is no such thing as downtime. This is serious business, and stock is needed for future shows.

They had taken a large booth at Summerside, and her daughter was manning a booth at an even bigger show in Halifax. The next weekend Bev and Terry were in Charlottetown for another fair. In fact, they are on the road to one fair or another for the six weeks prior to Christmas. As Terry says, it's a serious business where you have to focus for two months.

Bev started four years ago with vests, added baby bibs, tea towels with crocheted tops by Mom, crocheted dish clothes, then got requests for adult bibs and added aprons. Today they have a family business. Terry handles all administration and bookings. And, Bev chuckles, he likes to help the ladies try on the vests and aprons. Watching him I know she's correct; he holds purses and jackets, and positions the mirror so that they can get a good view of themselves. "I sew, do the design," Bev says.

Bev is a member of the Dartmouth Handcrafters' Guild, a fact that signals the quality of her creations. They pick their crafts fairs carefully. Terry says they like juried shows, "because you know that the quality of goods will attract a more upscale shopper — the kind who will buy the kind of items that Bev makes."

Two things triggered Bev to start her business. First was seeing a woman with a rack of vests at a craft fair, and thinking, "Too bad they're not reversible." The second was a sleep disorder. When unable to sleep, she sews. Her husband was very encouraging, and they held a contest in the family for the name of business. Soon it was time to go to market.

They tried three flea markets in Dartmouth to test the market and were received very well. Terry relates the story of the president of the Handcrafters' Guild seeing Bev's work.

"She said, 'You're too good to be here. You've gotta be in our show.'"
So Bev put her name on a wait list and did get a booth. This was her first
juried show, held at the Dartmouth Sportsplex.

"I was scared to death," says Bev. "We were swamped that first time,
worked around the clock. I had the drive and enough time then. Had
custom orders. I've learned to relax now," she grins.

They made $2,700 at that first show. It also drove home that Bev
had priced her wares too low. They had to take into account all expenses and costs and adjust their prices. They also had to learn about whole-
salers, and buying fabric. "I'm a fabric-aholic," she laughs.

Bev has worked hard to make her vests and other products stand
out as something special. "There are a lot of people sewing. I had to
do something different. So I do all of the doodads," she says, gestur-
ing to her own vest. "How many would put forty-seven buttons on a
vest?" Those buttons are part of the overall design of the piece, different and colourful, and they certainly give it a uniqueness seldom
found. Her attention to detail pays off, resulting in "an awful lot of
repeat orders."

Today her business is "more or less full time." But it gives her the
flexibility she needs. She will sew seven or eight days in a row, then can
take two, three, or more days off. The couple also take January and
February off, although they do use the time while travelling to purchase
fabric and other necessities. All in all, it's proven an excellent business
option for Bev, who still loves to sew.

"You really have to love doing it," says Bev Doman of small business. "When
it becomes a job you don't like, leave. I find this relaxing."

She also advocates getting help with the things you don't like doing. "I did
get help with the finances." She says she tried to learn as much as she could
about the bookkeeping end of things, even reading her daughter's books from
school on the subject. Now she jobs out the bookkeeping. "Every time I buy a
piece of fabric I write down on the receipt what it was. These are filed in a draw-
er ready to be taken to the bookkeeper."

Thinking of the Circuit?

One thing Bev and Terry ran into at this fair began a conversation about my dream. They had booked into a local hotel, which was also hosting a bluegrass festival. That translated into all-night jam sessions for the bluegrassers and no sleep for people who had to put in twelve hours dealing with the public at a craft fair the next day.

I desperately want to go heavier into craft fairs, travelling far and wide to take in events across the country. And I want to purchase a motorhome to go in. My thought is that we will have control of where we stay and what we eat. This is important to us for several reasons. First, Jack is diabetic, so it's much better being in control of his food and its preparation. Second, we can travel when dictated by weather. And we will be fulfilling my dream of travelling in a home on wheels. I love to be on the road, but admit to getting tired of lugging stuff in and out of hotels.

Another thing. We have a dog. She is the apple of our eye and we want her along, but we can't leave her in a car all day. We could, however, leave her for several hours in a motorhome — just as we leave her at home. So there you have the essence behind my next five-year plan.

That said, anyone thinking of going on the road in this way must take care to factor in *all* costs: gas to get there, accommodations, registration fee at the fair, any advertising or promo materials, bags, inventory. Then there are the one-time costs: the booth, drapes, stands, display racks, and decorations.

And think about the logistics of being at a fair. Traffic ebbs and flows. It seems you are either frantically making change or sitting trying to look alert and interested. Having two in a booth helps — you have someone to talk to and to spell you for a walk, bathroom break, or meal in the cafeteria.

Elfin Characters Down to Earth: Maria Heissler

Every so often you see something that makes you clasp your hands over your breast, take a deep breath, and sigh out with a full-hearted feeling. It's a feel-good thing. And it's the feeling I got when I saw Maria "Maia" Heissler's Down-To-Earth Creations. You see, I grew up believing in fairies and little people of the woodlands, and that created an immediate bond. I also have a passion for things made with natural findings.

Down-To-Earth Creations makes extensive use of natural, found, and recycled materials. Maia strives to offer unusual items inspired by nature, many with an accompanying story. The finest expression of her approach to creativity is seen in Maia's Forest Friend dioramas.

The Forest Friends are elfin creatures that dwell in southern Ontario woodlands. Each diorama captures a moment in the lives of these little people. Constructed around roots and knotholes, they incorporate

Ontario's Maia Heissler makes extensive use of natural, found, and recycled materials to create elfin characters in Forest Friends diorama.

everything from snail shells and birch bark to stones and edible wild plants. Each one-of-a-kind piece is signed, numbered, titled, and comes with an explanatory leaflet.

Maia, along with her writer/artist husband and three young sons, makes her home in the Murray Hills. The question that comes quickly to mind is, how did Maia come to dwell in this land of make-believe?

"My self-employed husband ran into some devastating roadblocks and all of a sudden there was virtually no income," she recalls. "With three sons to raise and a bleak economic outlook, I had to get something going. Some dabbling in market gardening to earn money led to jam-making, then candles and fudge and a lot of other things. I got out my calligraphy pens and made cards. Then, by chance, I showed someone the little people I had made a few years previous, but had given up on. She encouraged me to resurrect the idea (this was in 1994) and bit by bit, the Forest Friends gained in importance.

They've gone from taking up 10 percent of my booth space at a show to a good 75 percent."

She sells from craft shows and is working on a web site. "My dream is also to have a workshop separate from the house, a place where I can invite people to see my products. In the meantime, if someone has a special request, I happily send product through the mail."

As with all things, change is inevitable. As Maia's business evolves she makes wise use of things that others may have discarded. She also developed a series of craft manuals, which have become one of the staples of her business.

"I take pride in the extensive use of natural, found, and recycled materials. I have played with many natural materials, but found I couldn't do everything — focus has become increasingly important! — so, as I retired an idea from my inventory, I wrote it up in a craft manual. That's how *Wild Things on the Christmas Tree* came into being. There were so many ideas left over that I continued with *Wild Things for all Seasons* and eventually added *Wild Things in Envelopes*. At craft shows I sell milkweed pod stars and gnomes along with the manuals. What I consider to be the finest expression of my creativity is the 'Forest Friends.'"

This elfin civilization, born in Maia's imagination, has evolved beautifully over close to eighteen years, "propelled forward by a love for the woodlands, concern for the environment, a fascination with fairy tales, wonderful customer feedback, confirmations that I was on the right track, and, last but not least, a wild imagination.

"This part of my business now includes a self-published novel entitled *Look After the Little Ones*, greeting cards with photos of my dioramas, and the Forest Friend Lifestones, which are a bit like runes, but are symbols based on details from nature with accompanying life lessons."

Besides this she has developed her own recipe for a seasoning discovered in Quebec years ago. Maia's Salted Herbs is a growing part of her business. The accompanying recipe book is entitled *Down-To-Earth Cooking with Maia's Salted Herbs*.

She says she got into the business out of "sheer desperation at first, then through a mostly unshakable belief that this was the right thing." She was also was adamant about staying at home to raise her sons.

Doing the creative thing enabled her to accomplish that. "I have a passion for things made with natural findings."

Maia has met her challenges along the way, the biggest of which was, "Walking the economic tightrope! Working my way up to being able to get books printed, and to being able to afford the big shows. Realizing my dream of getting a workshop and reclaiming the house as a home. (Although a lot of people seem to like the atmosphere under this roof.) I have had to get through occasional moments of self-doubt. A challenge I have overcome is learning to find a focus, rather than trying to continue with a big variety. (And I do love dabbling in all kinds of things.) Balancing business with family can be tricky, but it's important."

Her best moments are undoubtedly seeing the incredible emotional reactions to her work and "connecting" with total strangers. "Knowing there are pieces of my work all over the world. Getting my first book published was huge."

The great times are, of course, tempered by the not quite so good. Things like missing birthdays and not having the house ready for Christmas, "and having to drive through Toronto by myself when my husband was doing extra work on a movie set. I don't like the city and I don't like big highways."

Never one to rest on her laurels, Maia is planning an expanded book of "woodland reflections" based on her Forest Friend Lifestones. She is also working with one of her brothers to expand Maia's Salted Herbs. And then there is that workshop and showroom.

"There is a producer in Toronto who still dreams of making *Look After the Little Ones* into a live action/animated movie. That would be incredible!"

Maia may dwell in a land of fantasy when she is creating her Forest Friends, but when it comes to business she offers down-to-earth advice: "Choose something for which you can have a passion, something you can believe in. Believe in yourself. *Focus.* Above all, never give up! I believe firmly in a combination of passion and compassion: passion for what you do and compassion for the people you have to deal with."

Bookbinders Open for Visits: La Tranchefile

Economuseum, a Canadian government initiative designed to stimulate entrepreneurship, showcases artisans and art trades by designating businesses that use authentic techniques or know-how as Economuseums. These entrepreneurs must fund their business by sale of their products and respect quality standards to stay in the network. They are wonderful places to visit and see artisans at work.

One such business, operated by Odette Drapeau, Isabelle Chasse, and Patrick Grimond, fits right in with our focus on artisans, for these folks are bookbinders. As you walk into La Tranchefile in Montreal, you are enveloped by the fine perfume of leather. Here you can discover the vitality of a traditional craft that explores very contemporary forms of expression. The artisans use canvas bindings, shagreen bindings, guest books, handmade paper, gold-leaf gilding, and *savoir faire* that protects and honours manuscripts and memories. They adapt their creativity to each new project, whether for unique objects or mass production. The boutique offers the public a range of objects at a variety of prices as well as a customized bookbinding service to suit every pocketbook.

La Tranchefile organizes exhibitions several times a year on the theme of artistic bookbinding and takes part in many special events. They also offer training courses.

Flower Mosaics Heart's Ease Creations: Wendy Alkins Pobjoy

"There is peace in these fresh-picked blossoms. They charm the mind into serenity. Their sweet lines and sensuous forms can be a wonderful antidote to stress. Allow your eyes to travel their glowing curves, rays and spirals and to explore their unexpected vistas," says Wendy Alkins Pobjoy.

When Wendy needed a birthday gift for her daughter she turned to her garden, camera in hand. The clematis and pansies were blooming, her creative juices were flowing, and soon the first flower mosaic, a visually stunning photograph of artfully arranged flower blossoms, was born. Her gift received great accolades from those who saw it, so she created a few more over the course of the summer.

Prince Edward Island's Wendy Alkins Pobjoy creates flower mosaics from her garden, which she markets through Heart's Ease Creations.

"It wasn't until over the winter that I started believing that I had a product, something that people would actually pay for. I think it's because when the real flowers are gone, the ones I had captured were so entrancing, so alive looking, in the flower mosaic."

By the next summer the artisan was in full-time business, naming Heart's Ease Creations after the wild pansy.

"Most pansies and violets have been called heartsease, from time to time over the centuries. Johnny Jump-ups are what I imagine. The word 'heart's-ease' also means 'peace of mind, tranquillity,' which is what I wish for us all."

In fact, she says, "The thing that pleases me the most in terms of response from people is that they say 'you are selling joy.' There is an emotional response to the pictures. I feel that as I'm involved in their creation, but others also feel that they are calming and bring joy. I couldn't ask more than people feeling that."

While some customers just get grabbed by an image as they walk by, others have a room or friend's room in mind and are looking for specific colour combinations. If they don't find it the first time around they should just wait a while. Wendy continues to create and to expand her product lines. She is also, she says, in awe of how differently her art is interpreted by individuals.

"I have a line of fairies that I do. It amazes me how some people see them, others don't, yet those people get an uplift anyway. So fascinating."

The flowers in her images grow in her gardens at home near Belle River, Prince Edward Island. She spends many hours choosing, planting, starting seed.

"For weeks I grow dozens of seedlings all over the house and greenhouse, until the weather gets warm. Then I plant them out and water, feed, and weed them 'til they bloom. I pick the blossoms at the peak of their glory, then arrange and photograph them while they are fresh and vibrant."

She refers to her creations as mosaics because the process is similar to tiling in placing pieces of the whole.

"I have to put flowers, or even petals, down one at a time and the process reminded me of working with ceramic tiles."

Wendy began selling her work through the farmers' market and twelve stores, on consignment over the summer. Even in what has been deemed a "slow season" those shopkeepers said her artistic matted photographs did well.

"The farmers' market has been a wonderful market investigation tool," she says. "Responses so encouraging. People are going there for cabbages and potatoes. To see someone passing by and literally get grabbed, the eyes drawn to the images is very encouraging, very supportive, invaluable."

She broadened her marketing by attending her first Christmas craft fair and has developed a catalogue for mail-order sales.

"As soon as I have the craft fairs under my belt my attention is going to be to on getting my web site functioning properly. Right now it's just a communication with customers already established," she laughs. "Being one person doing everything, it's just not possible to get everything done."

That site will eventually be built into an on-line catalogue for mail-order sales. She doesn't envision having a shop at home, at least not now. An avid gardener, Wendy had thought years ago that she would like to have a nursery. "But I found myself literally running around the place with a baby on my hip. I would spend so many hours working in the garden and hardly anyone would see them. This is a way to share with people beyond my garden."

Mail Order Appealing Sales Tool

Mail order is a concept that many home business owners see as an appealing sales method. The vision of cheques arriving in the mail, requiring one to simply mail away goods, is an enticing one. However, like other types of direct selling, creating a successful mail-order business requires a great deal of marketing finesse and dedication to the task at hand. Many small businesses use mail order as one of several ways to increase sales. So, too, can anyone with a product to sell use marketing through mail order as one means of making her business skyrocket. Unless you have a tremendous amount of money to invest you must start small and work to grow your business. Here are a few easy tips:

- Select products to test market with care: Mail-order items should be unique, meet people's needs, mail well, fit into impulse buying, be reliable and well made, and be priced competitively.
- Develop your own mailing list: As soon as you decide to put mail order into your future, begin developing a mailing list. Include family, friends, everyone you know who might be interested in your product. If you have a booth at a trade or craft show, have a draw for a prize, giving ballots to those who show an interest in your product. Ask current customers if they would like your catalogue to go to any of their friends. You can buy or rent mailing lists, but seek the advice of experts before paying out big dollars. Make sure the list is targeted to people who will have an interest in your product.
- Establish a target market: Decide where you feel the best potential lies for mail order, e.g. small business owners, skiers, pet owners, car buffs, or gourmet cooks.

- Place small, inexpensive ads in publications of interest to your target market: A young fellow we know had great success selling his handmade goose calls through small classified ads in a hunting magazine. Check a good magazine store and your library (ask for assistance and they will provide you with listings of publications), as well as business service centres.

- Plan the timing of your first promotion: The following months are considered the best for mail-order sales: January, February, September, October, and November. However, if your product is geared to a specific activity or time of year — such as gardening, or icy weather — time your promotion accordingly.

- Word your ads and catalogues carefully: Check out successful companies for how they do it and read up on attention-grabbing wording and phrases.

- Print small quantities of catalogues or promotional material: Don't do big print runs until you have had time to test the effectiveness of your material. Always have clear instructions on how to order and an order form included in your material.

- Set aside time to grow: Mail-order businesses take time and perseverance to develop. Give yourself both.

- Dedicate space to storage of your product and mailing operation: In short, be organized and ready for orders to come in.

- Mail order is a form a direct selling, made a little easier for those who dislike face-to-face pitching.

Silkscreeners, Partners: Doreen Smith and Tjamkje Lootsma

After more than fifteen years in business, silkscreeners Doreen Smith and Tjamkje (Chum) Lootsma took stock and realized they could step back and stay in the same place. The duo own and operate Dmajor Fabric Studio Ltd. in Winsloe, Prince Edward Island. Smith designs and sews while Lootsma hand-cuts stencils and prints on natural-fibre clothing and household items, using environmentally friendly inks.

They describe their lives as a happy collaboration of an organic gardener (Lootsma) and an artist (Smith), with a passion for nature that is reflected in their designs.

To understand what makes their work stand out in a world where T-shirts are churned out thousands at a time, one must consider the difference between a fully mechanized printing machine, which can whip through eighty or ninety dozen T-shirts an hour, and a hand operation, which produces twenty to forty a day using original designs and water-soluble inks that contain no benzines or varsols, making them as environmentally friendly as they can get. Heat processing makes their products washable.

The path that led these women to a silkscreening career is an interesting one. Smith was teaching art at junior high when her classes got too large.

"I don't know if you ever tried to teach thirty kids with woodcutting tools and such in their hands," she laughs, "but I didn't want to be part of it." She left in 1982, took some classes, and started building a silkscreen studio.

Lootsma left Ontario to buy a camping supply store and live an outdoor lifestyle. She quickly found the store kept her indoors more than she'd bargained for and turned to organic gardening.

The two met at the farmers' market and began helping each other. Smith pulled Lootsma's weeds. Lootsma held Smith's screens. Soon Smith was running out of room. Lootsma realized it was taking too much time and energy to make a few pennies.

"Each piece had to be ironed to set the inks, that meant ironing every night. It pushed us into realizing we had to do something."

They called the Ontario Crafts Council for help sourcing an oven to set the inks and began searching for a larger space. The oven forced the issue — it needed a lot of room because of the heat. Smith knew she had to locate somewhere affordable where she would be comfortable working day or night.

"So her eyes lit on my bungalow," said Lootsma with a wry grin. In 1986 a builder was called in. The original home became the studio, and two-storey living quarters were added.

Lootsma was still planning to garden while Smith printed. Then came a fateful knock on the door; their visitor bore a very large order.

"We couldn't turn it down — Chum learned to print fast! At the end of that year, we were not gardening to sell anymore," says Smith, recalling a few lean times in the beginning.

"When you wholesale, it takes a while for money to trickle in. We went to the Atlantic Crafts Trade Show, got more orders, added Christmas shows, and the business grew. It became obvious we could have a steadier income year round with printing. And, it's not as hard on the back as gardening!"

In 1995, they added on again. A garage and a wide hall connected to the studio made attending shows easier and facilitated opening a seasonal shop. They could dolly things into their van without going outside. Display material, kept in the garage, could also be comfortably loaded — especially appreciated during P.E.I. winters!

"What a difference that made!" The hall serves as a display area for their shop. A clearance bin at the back is always popular. "People really enjoy that clearance bin. We had boxes of things that didn't sell at shows. Couldn't offer it as new product, so this is a good way to clear old stock."

Opening their shop, and experiencing its success, led to re-evaluation. They determined to balance, to cut back on shows. "We used to do as many as ten each year, with one ten-day show in Ottawa."

Asked when their business started to make money, they look at each other and answer in unison, "When we stopped doing shows." In the beginning they lived off shows, but today they say the bottom-line figures, as well as the downtime and the hard work of preparation, change that.

"Our experience is you have to have so much stock. At a ten-day show you have to ensure the booth looks as full on the tenth day as the first. That means producing a large amount of stock, packing, having it shipped, driving to Ottawa, hotel expenses, and the cost of the show. It was just too expensive."

Their objective now is to make things that may take a bit more time, but are more fun. "Just to get out of the production mode. Even by cutting shows we relieved the pressure," says Smith, joking that they are getting older.

This desire to get back to their creative roots led them to add a new art form, Shibori, an ancient Japanese fabric decorating technique described as the inventive art of shaped, resistance dying or discharging of colour. The cloth is manipulated to create abstract repeat patterns.

Their ever-evolving product line includes more than forty designs applied to T-shirts, scoop-neck shirts, and sweatshirts, shawls, aprons, seven different kinds of bags, tea towels, and cushions. The designs are Dmajor's showpiece. A one-word description would have to be "nature," but it doesn't begin to encompass the broad scope of birds, flowers, and distinct Prince Edward Island and Atlantic Canadian images they have created. For Chum and Doreen, an important element in what they do is the fun and enjoyment that they can share through Dmajor. So committed are they to quality, they have concealed a hidden music note as a signature on each and every one of their products.

Doreen Smith and Chum Lootsma of Dmajor Fabric Studio Ltd. freely offer advice for those starting out in business: "Be sure you really like what you are doing. It's more important than a business plan. Not according to bankers maybe but ... People have no concept of what it means to do everything. We tell them you have to be the sales clerk, shipper, packager, producer, marketer. You have to source and order your supplies. That can be very time-consuming and trying especially when something new or specific. And make friends with a banker!"

Image Can Be Everything
Anyone in any business needs to be aware of the image they project, and nowhere is it easier to fall into the trap of thinking anything goes than in the arts and crafts fields. It is especially important to be aware that people associate the quality of your product with the person they see.

Take some steps to make sure that you are benefitting the most from the image you present to potential customers (and remember, everyone you meet is a potential customer):

- Define what your image should be. An artist can benefit from a far different look than someone working in a high-tech corporate environment.
- Once you decide on your image, develop or review your print materials, such as business cards, brochures, and signage, to make sure they reinforce it.
- Think through every public appearance, meeting, class you teach, networking opportunity, or trade or craft show. These face-to-face activities, more than anything else, instill your image in the minds of potential clients.

Sew Much Fun Sharing the Skills: Linda MacPhee

Another individual who has turned her love of fabric and fashion into a business, but on a much larger scale, is Linda MacPhee of Edmonton, creator and host of *Sew Much Fun*, a popular television series. According to her web site, www.macpheeworkshop.com, and to the 2003 Edmonton Woman Consumer Guide, Linda is a leading innovator in the clothing design and home sewing industry, and she is well known across Canada as the co-founder of MacPhee Workshop, one of Canada's largest design houses and pattern manufacturers, celebrating over twenty years in business.

In her capacity as creative director and chief fashion designer, she has been instrumental in developing and producing over two hundred patterns. Prior to her television show's North American success, she produced five critically acclaimed sewing videos. Linda successfully combines good design with quality fabrics to produce a line of custom-designed clothing and patterns with a distinctive personal flair.

Among the innovative offerings from MacPhee Workshop are sewing retreats, an opportunity to spend two whole days (and one evening) sewing and socializing with kindred spirits! Just think: no cooking, no cleaning, nobody to entertain, nobody to pick up after — just you and your machine creating wonderful garments. Participants take their own machines and materials. The workshops provide the space, meals, and instructors in a great setting — perfect for a sewing extravaganza and a perfect example of the innovative thinking that brought her recognition through the Canadian Awards for Business Excellence and a nomination as Woman Entrepreneur of the Year.

Northwest Coast Design, a Story of Evolution: Sabina Hill

Vancouver designer Sabina Hill, of Sabina Hill Northwest Coast Design, works with invited First Nations artists to create custom furniture, art pieces, and accessories that combine the rich mythology of Northwest Coast aboriginal culture with a contemporary design aesthetic.

Her work is presented in limited and open edition collections, or through commissioned pieces for individual clients. All limited edition pieces are authenticated by an inlaid engraved logo and a certificate that indicates the edition number. Sabina's design philosophy of focusing on creating works that capture the essence of Pacific Northwest Coast culture has created a very successful niche for her work. How did she get there?

Photo courtesy of John Watson.

Eagle wall panel created by Sabina Hill of Vancouver's Sabina Hill Northwest Coast Design with Steve Smith (tribal affiliation: Kwakwaka'wakn). It utilizes solid Douglas Fir, glass, and black anodized aluminum with stainless steel standoffs.

161

Collaborating with talented First Nations artists to create pieces that are a unique fusion of contemporary modern and traditional Northwest Coast aesthetics has been part of Sabina's evolution. An honours graduate of the University of British Columbia School of Architecture, she founded Sabina Hill Design in 1993, a company that specializes in renovations and custom-designed homes, landscape design, and built-in furniture.

Sabina first approached Corrine Hunt, a highly regarded designer of Northwest Coast native jewellery from Alert Bay, with the concept of integrating First Nations motifs with contemporary furniture designs. They co-founded HillHunt, a joint venture to create limited edition custom furniture and art pieces by combining the rich history and culture of the aboriginal design with a contemporary aesthetic.

This fusion of their disciplines grew from Sabina's desire to incorporate West Coast Native motifs into more than wall hangings and other ornaments and Hunt's desire to add functionality to her Native art. Furniture provided a good canvas, as it has with such traditional Native creations as bentwood boxes. Several collections were designed and produced, which included coffee and side tables, a bench, and other custom designs using maple and cherry wood and incorporating Native motifs cut into stainless steel and aluminium.

Sabina would come to the table with the concept and design while Corrine worked with the motif. They put art to work by combining traditional aboriginal design with contemporary furniture to create usable household decor while "bringing the ceremonial into daily life."

After working together for several years, they have again seen change and today have evolved to operate separate businesses. Corrine is focusing on her jewellery design. Sabina is collaborating with First Nations artist Steve Smith in her new Formlines Collection, which features solid hardwoods and precision-cut metal and glass incorporating evolving colours and unique finishes and wood veneers.

By integrating First Nations motifs in her designs, Sabina creates pieces that are uniquely expressive of her West Coast home.

Brand Thyself

A few years back we were all told we had to create an image for ourselves and for our businesses if we wanted to attain success. Today the buzzword is brand.

So what is this branding concept? It is the perception that clients and potential customers have of you and your products. It is the promise of value that will be received. The experts tell us that you need to understand and be able to articulate these things to others in a concise, short manner before you spend a lot of time developing print material, logos, and things that project your image.

They also say the strongest "brand" will enable stakeholders to keep focused on the mandate and present it to others in a concise way, much as a mission statement does.

To create a brand, a business needs to examine their "promise" to their clients and then define it in words and images. You should end up with a short description of the business — say fifty to sixty words, no more — and a tag line or slogan of just a few words to use, for example, on a business card or letterhead. The next step could be a logo. But be careful with this one. Perhaps some images to use consistently are all you need.

I have a personal dislike of anything called a logo that has to be explained. If someone has to interpret it for you, ditch it, unless you have major dollars to spend imprinting it on consumers' minds. I was once at a presentation where they unveiled a logo designed to "brand" a line of products. It took the designers twenty minutes to explain what all the squiggles and lines represented — and we were an audience who had already been introduced to the campaign, had been hearing about it for months in fact. What a waste of time and money!

With or without a logo, once you have defined your brand and have gone through the process of refining it until you are happy with it, the real work begins. You must manage it well to provide continuity to your vision and how you and your business are presented. All communication material must be expressive of the brand as you have defined it. This means paying constant attention to where, when, and how the brand is presented. If branding is something you want to bring to your business, approach your professional associations and government support agencies for guidance. It is important to do this job properly and to be prepared for the commitment of time, energy, and creativity to both develop and manage your brand.

Worthy of Note

- I met artist Marilyn Tucker at a craft fair and was impressed by her products, which combined heritage and beauty while encouraging her customers to utilize their creative skills. She began constructing fabric wall hangings in 1983. Today she is known for designing Fairwind Embroidery kits. Marilyn has developed a unique way to create the traditional embroidery kits. The background design is silkscreened with water-soluble inks on fabric. The embroiderer embellishes the picture by using embroidery thread to give the completed piece depth and movement. Among the offerings of Fairwind Embroidery of St. John's, Newfoundland, are kits licensed by the Art Gallery of Nova Scotia and based on original paintings by Maud Lewis, one of Nova Scotia's most famous folk artists. Marilyn Tucker has completed several visual arts courses at the Memorial University of Newfoundland and is currently a member of the St. John's Guild of Embroiderers.

Chapter Eight:
It's a Family Affair

There is a special pleasure to be enjoyed when sharing an interest, a common passion in a business with a loved one. Not only are these the folks that we trust, know best, and feel secure with, but there is also a very heartwarming feeling in knowing that our own benefit from our labours. It's the truth behind keeping it in the family.

Julie V. Watson

Family businesses are a vital part of Canada's economy. They generate 45 percent of the GOP, according to *Soho Magazine*'s spring 2003 issue. They are responsible for 70 percent of all new jobs and employ 4.7 million people full-time and 1.3 million part-time. In 1999, family businesses generated sales worth $1.3 trillion.

Of course, many of these businesses are far bigger players than the focus of this book. We are more interested in smaller businesses, wife and husband, mother and child, daughter and parent.

It isn't always easy, but for those who find the formula to make it work in their unique situation, a family business can provide a lifestyle that is hard to equal.

Dog Paddling Adventures: Kathryn Howell

If you are a dog lover, as I am, the idea of a vacation adventure where my beloved Tipsy is welcomed with open arms is just too cool.

"The goal of Dog Paddling Adventures is to provide a wonderful outdoor experience for both you and your dog, and our passion for the animals of the earth and their habitat will enhance each of our trips in a unique and special way," says Kathryn Howell.

Kathryn was quick to recognize a way to combine things that she and her husband love and enjoy, as well as the individual strength areas they have, to develop a business that has proven to be a great success.

"My husband and I had always been into

Dog Paddling Adventures combines business with love for the outdoors and pets in a true family affair. Kathryn Howell, the driving force behind the business, says the key to success is working "together."

adventure travel (and had hoped to open our own outdoor adventure company one day). Eren was an outdoor adventure guide for several years when we met and as soon as we got our puppy Jessie he began taking her on canoe trips with him. After their first trip he told me how wonderful it was to share the great outdoors with her and that he could never imagine another trip without her. As soon as he said that the ideas started flowing in my mind and I said that's it! We have to start a company that takes people and their dogs out on adventure outdoor based trips! I knew that people loved being with their dogs and that there were so few places that allowed let alone welcomed your dog to join you, especially on vacations. As soon as the idea was born I immediately starting working on a web site, brochures and attending pet shows and from there it simply flourished!"

She says the web site was very important and has proven to be their key tool in reaching dog lovers around the world. "People love reading about our trips and viewing the gallery (the photos of the dogs are so much fun), the pet shows were great too. It was the perfect way to meet tons of local dog lovers like ourselves and show them what we had to offer and explain all about our trips."

They started off just offering summer canoe trips, but quickly the demand was greater for one-day adventures and weekend trips all throughout the year, so they started their Dog Lovers Spring and Fall Hiking Clubs, and then added on winter skijoring trips as well.

"Kathryn, the business personality and driving force behind Dog Paddling Adventures, has obtained her animal first aid certificate and is the trip photographer and co-chef. She is the friendly voice and smiling face on the other end of your emails, and is always up for a good doggy story around camp," says their web site, dogpaddlingadventures.com.

Kathryn Howell shares her advice on working together as a couple, saying, "The most important part is working 'together'! Knowing whose qualities are best at each aspect of the business. For Eren and I — he is an amazing outdoor guide and leader and while I love the trips my best qualities are in the office, I love dealing with the clients, booking the trips and marketing our company. So as a team it works fantastic. Eren has amazing ideas on trips and gear and guides and after he comes up with the ideas I go about marketing and selling them.

"It's very important to decide who will take care of what when you are partners with your spouse so that you each know what responsibilities are yours and so that you lean on each other to know what's best for their part of the business.

"We enjoy our 'staff meetings' too where we sit down and brainstorm and go through what needs to be done and how to go about it. Even though we both have our areas of expertise we always have great thoughts and ideas on other stuff as well and it's amazing how much brainstorming you can get done when you devote an afternoon to it! Working together as a team and appreciating one another's ideas and knowledge really allows you to appreciate each other and work great together!"

On Getting Into Adventure Tourism

"Well the best thing is to find a niche, something that people are looking for or really can relate to," says Kathryn Howell of Dog Paddling Adventures. "There are a lot of outdoor adventure companies that offer canoeing and hiking tours but none of them allow dogs so we are truly unique, which makes the marketing aspect much easier and really helps you to stand out on the web.

"If you can find a concept that either offers something new or different or a new and unique way of going about adventure travel your web site becomes much easier to find on search engines and your name gets out there a lot faster than if you are similar to all the other existing companies.

"It's also really important to get great guides on your team. We make sure to only hire guides who have a lot of outdoor experience as well as a passion for not only the outdoors but dogs as well. Your guides are your team and they represent your company and your image, if clients feel comfortable with them and enjoy their company they recommend you to their friends etc and word of mouth is very important.

"Quality of products is also key, we made sure to get all new equipment that was perfectly suited for our clientele, knowing your clients is very important. We knew that a lot of our clientele would be from the city and may have never done an outdoor trip before so we made sure to have comfortable and roomy tents (especially since clients share with their four-legged friends), sleeping pads for extra comfort, delicious meals, big sturdy boats, and all the gear they need so that they don't have to bring anything with them.

"Making an experience really just that an 'experience' is so important for people. Often people book an adventure trip because they want to try something they have never done before, whether it is paddling or hiking or skiing and they want to feel like they really had an adventure. On our trips we make sure they feel that way. We start all of our trips whether they are one day or longer with a full instruction of whatever that trip is about.

"We teach them how to paddle so that they really feel like they have learned something by the end of their trip. We also show them how we put up the tents, make our meals, use our gear, etc. By the end of a Dog Paddling Trip clients are nice and tired (as well as relaxed) and they really feel like they have learned a lot and had a truly outdoor experience.

"Going the extra mile is also important for clients. On each of our trips we take tons of photos of the group and of the clients and their pups. After the trip we send them a thank you letter along with photos of them and their dog and a group shot in a little doggy album that has their dog's name engraved on the front. (We also put the best photos on our web site on a web page that has their trip date and name on the top so they can check it out and show family and friends.) Things like this really mean a lot to the clients and make you stand out above the rest."

Keeper of the Castle: Linda Paoli Steele

After varied careers, Linda Paoli Steele fulfilled every child's fantasy and bought herself a castle. In fact, she and her family got themselves several castles at Woodleigh Replicas in Burlington, Prince Edward Island.

The grounds at this major tourist attraction feature thirty large-scale replicas. During World War I, Ernest Johnstone determined to duplicate the beauty found in England and Scotland. Returning home, he landscaped farmland to resemble Britain's manicured parks. Following service in World War II, Lieutenant Colonel Johnstone and his son, Archie, also a war veteran, built replicas of some of Britain's most famous buildings and castles.

By 1958, visitors were arriving in such numbers that the grounds were officially opened to the public, attracting over two million people. Today's site includes extensive gardens, fountains, food services, a gift shop, a picnic area and playground, and a staff of thirty to keep it all working. Some replicas, large enough to enter, are furnished with antiques and artifacts.

The Steeles' expertise provides the skilled care needed to maintain and operate a complex property.

"My husband, Peter, and I have been in business since 1976, in property development, construction, and restoration," says Linda, who also worked in the museum and publishing fields for many years. "My first venture in tourism was a large accommodations property, where I learned hands-on about the industry. What appealed to me about Woodleigh was the beauty of the property and the perfect fit for my interests and experience, and those of the family. We now have three generations working here."

She says the most enjoyable part of the business has been the enormous satisfaction of improving and overseeing the gardens and grounds of the forty-acre park. That learning curve has been short and steep.

"The fact that Mother Nature throws many unexpected curves can be the frustrating at times. From a strictly business point of view, the short tourism season presents the most difficulties."

As well as operating and maintaining the replicas and gardens, Linda, Peter, and daughter Jennifer host several special events, including a six-week Medieval Faire, a Highland Games, and, at Christmas, Light Up the Castles.

When asked if she has any words of wisdom to share, Linda said she thinks the most valuable trait in small business is perseverance.

"As for family business, I would recommend that people try to separate times and occasions for family relationships, apart from the business. The tendency is for the business to swallow up the family, or at least for the two to interweave themselves too much. So, in our case, spouse-only time, mother-daughter time, and grandmother-grandchildren time is very important."

Find Time for You — Your Most Important Asset

We hear a lot about time management, usually directed at getting the most business done in the shortest time. But wait, your most important asset — you — needs its own time, one of the hardest elements to come by in each day for WIBs. By the time you run your business, take care of your family, and keep the household running smoothly it's difficult to find time for you.

Without it you probably won't be able to sustain the high level of accomplishment that leads to ongoing success.

Prioritize, and include time for yourself. Make sure it's relaxing time to allow your batteries to recharge.

Schedule break time between tough tasks, especially meetings or negotiations. It gives the brain a chance to switch focus and increases energy levels.

Look at the tasks ahead of you, decide what you must do yourself and what you can delegate — then do it.

Empower others to share the workload by slowly introducing them to decisions they can make. Work with them while they learn, then trust them to master what needs to be done.

Don't forget to vocalize praise and recognition for a job well done, whether by you or those working with you. It's really important to acknowledge yourself when you have done a good job.

If your life has evolved into one where every minute is controlled by your appointment book, then schedule in a walk, games with the kids, dinner with your significant other, meals (it's amazing how many of us skip those!), relaxing activities of your choice, and, most important of all, sleep time.

World's Only Plasma Defroster: Marjorie E. Stevenson-Dawson

Marjorie E. Stevenson-Dawson is vice-president, COO, and chief marketing executive of ARK Bio-Medical Canada Corp. "The COO," she smiles, "basically means if it has to be done, do it. It covers the whole gamut of operations from service to sales to purchasing to accounting, and the list goes on."

ARKBIO, in Winsloe, Prince Edward Island, manufactures the only FDA 510K Microwave Plasma Defroster in the world, with over twenty international distributors selling to more than fifty countries. Marjorie and her partner/husband established ARKBIO in 1995 after she researched the American market. Over twenty-five years' experience provided a solid track record in sales, marketing, human resources, and public relations.

"I found it necessary to develop significant knowledge in microelectronics and software development to work with engineering and purchasing divisions in our production and R&D departments.

"ARKBIO works directly with customers in North America in all aspects of sales and service. Detailed knowledge of the changing face of consolidation and ever increasing HMO organizations in the U.S. has been a paramount requirement. Because our product deals with one component of blood I had to obtain a diversified base of medical knowledge as it pertains to blood and its collection, separation, preservation, and delivery."

Her biggest personal challenge has been, she says, "Keeping abreast of the ever changing technology and being informed enough to decide if it should, or could, be incorporated into the business. Being always aware of individual circumstances of each client relating to regulatory changes, their technological usage in-house, and constant changes in customer contacts."

Two challenges to the business are raising growth capital and finding team players with the dedication and work ethic needed in an international business dealing with so many different countries and cultures. It is a business that demands adaptability and a higher level of customer service because of limited face-to-face interaction.

Marjorie has always worked in areas that have a positive impact on the world around her at the human level.

"Years spent working with scientific research in areas that would see development of new medical devices with potential to make a significant contribution to lifesaving situations was extremely influential."

Marjorie E. Stevenson-Dawson says it is a wonderful time for women to be in business. "The opportunities are only as limited as one's personal abilities, attitude, and ambitions. The natural nature of the female to nurture is a valuable resource to a business she has an ownership relationship in.

"Success stories of women in business should be used as confidence builders for a new generation of female entrepreneurs to take steps into the world with a confidence that they can meet the challenges that the business world has to offer and with the right mental attitude surpass even their own expectations."

Movin' Upscale: Donna Oseen

Donna Oseen's family business definitely has some great moves. DLO Move Support Services Ltd., of North Vancouver, British Columbia, is making a major mark in the corporate world as the business to call when going from Point A to Point B.

DLO is committed to helping clients maintain a sense of order and normalcy while executing a well-timed, supervised, and seamless move. A smooth transfer of employees and equipment is not only good for productivity and employee morale, it is also necessary to prevent lost revenues and high costs and to maintain client connections.

Donna had already made her mark as an organizing guru when she got into the moving business. As the manager of services and facilities at a firm of over one hundred lawyers, her responsibilities included anything that needed to be moved, changed, fixed, faxed, copied, or supplied. In the course of her work she often turned to her son, Lane, who had developed expertise in many such matters.

Thinking a second career was in order, Donna embarked on a new venture when she started her own company with Lane. DLO provides a wide range of services, including equipment analysis, repairs, maintenance, and the many things required to keep an office in great shape. For a time she worked part-time for DLO and part-time for the law firm.

In just six years DLO saw its business grow by 25 percent a year, resulting in a hand-picked staff of over thirty-five movers to help meet the growing demand. Now one of the major players in Vancouver's corporate moving game, they deal with high-profile clients who seek help with relocation, expansion, and equipment set-up. Today Donna is known as a founding partner and the Director of Move Coordination and Facilities Management Services.

Donna has built the business using extensive hands-on experience with all aspects of office management, which provided her with the insight to help clients improve the overall efficiency of their operations. Her expertise extends beyond coordinating the move, minimizing disruption, and eliminating downtime. Her human resources background enables her to motivate staff to involve themselves in the process in a positive way, and broader management experience allows her to identify improvements to work processes, introduce new effi-ciencies, and capitalize on the marketing and repositioning opportu-nities afforded by the move.

A large corporate move takes anywhere from three to six months of planning and organization. The company works from a hundred-point checklist for everything from changing phone numbers, postal codes, and letterhead to telephone and computer system disconnection and hookup. Smaller moves need the same attention to detail, even though less time is required.

Strict hiring policies, uniformed movers, and attention to the con-cerns and needs of a clientele that includes many professional firms who are concerned about image and the security of their equipment and information base are an important part of DLO's policy.

"The gentlemen who wear our uniforms are ambassadors for our company and are professional, clean cut, technically skilled individuals who are compatible with client's office environment."

The heart of the business today, because of client demands, has become the corporate moving division. "We started out doing whatever the client needed to make their office work and realized the moving was the biggest aspect," says Laurie Oseen, Lane's wife.

Some media have been comparing the management team roster to a well-cast prime-time sitcom cast: mom Donna, partner and son Lane, as well as Lane's wife, Laurie, and sister, Analise. It truly is a family affair.

One of the most important and satisfying skills Donna acquired in her early days as an administrator was how to work with people and create a team. She credits her optimistic outlook — seeing the glass half full — for her success in working with people.

The team that is at the helm of DLO is a family, and she says they always have to be careful of one another's feelings. "We communicate and we trust each other." And, she points out, Lane has the biggest challenge: he works with his mother, his sister, and his wife.

Surprise! You're Wealthy — Financial Success

The disquieting results of a women's investor poll conducted for a division of TD Bank Financial Group led Patricia Lovett-Reid to publish *Surprise! You're Wealthy*, addressing the financial planning needs of women. The survey found that almost half the women interviewed did not consider themselves to be knowledgeable investors. Close to 40 percent of the women lacked confidence in their ability to manage their own investments, and approximately 50 percent of them considered themselves to be low-risk investors.

Many factors impact a woman's financial situation: inheritance, divorce, lottery winning, insurance settlements, even a separation package due to an employer downsizing, and of course women entrepreneurs are finding success leading to financial independence and becoming wealthy. Unfortunately, many women are not equipped to effectively manage their finances.

"In my opinion," says Lovett-Reid, "it's neglect that leads people astray. Procrastination is one of the biggest obstacles to financial well-being." Among the things that should not be neglected is keeping pace with economic advances.

"The most important educational initiatives for women to take are learning income and wealth management. At the end of the day your goals need to be specific so that you can easily determine whether you are falling short, and be specific in what you need to do."

Patricia Lovett-Reid says the most important things women can do are create their own opportunities and sell themselves or their ideas. Her keys to success:

- Having a bit of optimism — if you can truly believe another door will open it will, but it's only going to happen if you create opportunity.
- The most important educational initiatives for women to take are learning income and wealth management.

- You have to play on areas that enhance your strengths. I often hear women say, "I have to take a course." I ask why are you doing that if it is not something you like. Take a course in something you are good at and get better at it. Play to your strengths. Have a bit of courage. At the end of the day your goals need to be specific so that you can easily determine whether you are falling short, and be specific in what you need to do.

Good luck!

Teeing Off Keeps Family Biz on Course: Merina Currie

Merina Currie and her husband own and operate Glen Afton Golf Course (18 holes, par 70) located on the south shore of Prince Edward Island, a beautiful location overlooking Northumberland Strait. Merina looks look after management of the pro shop, staff, advertising, supplies, and accounting. Her husband, Harley Currie, looks after superintending, the grounds, etc. "Our office is at home, so after I leave the pro shop, I do the office work at home."

Their entry into the golf business came through family.

"My husband's father, Delmar Currie, started the golf course around twenty-five years ago; he passed away seven years ago and left it to my husband [Harley] and his brother; we bought out his brother's share four years ago, and here we are. This being our fourth year, we have been able to make quite a few changes and are very much enjoying being owners and operators as a team of husband and wife."

Prior to entering the golf business, Merina worked for many years for the local college and, before that, the provincial government.

"It's quite a change owning and operating your own business. I would never want to work for someone else again. There are pros and cons, of course, but the grass is definitely greener on this side." The best part, she says, is not having to live up to someone else's rules, but rather "making and breaking your own rules" as needed.

"Creativity is such a wonderful thing, and learning as you go is amazing. I really believe in a saying my father told me many years ago, 'If there's a will, there's a way,' and another told me by Dr. Don Glendenning, former president of Holland College, 'It's a lot easier to get forgiveness than permission.'"

The couple believe in giving back, and say a special thing about owning Glen Afton is that it enables them to give memberships each year to adults or juniors who love golfing but can't afford it. "It seems that someone comes along each year that I hear about and I just love doing it." This year it went to a father and his two sons. "The look on their faces is something I won't forget. Their 'hand-drawn' thank-you card is priceless and is on my desk at all times. Life is about what you do and what you give. Another special thing is the 'members' that come back every year. They're like our extended family. In the spring, it's so exciting to see everyone. There's always lots of hugs and joking going around. Our pro shop is very family and friend oriented, and the staff working with us are fun and loving. Some of our family work at the golf course and we have students who come back each year. We care about people. We have many visitors from off-Island that come every summer, many are on a first-name basis."

Two years ago they started the Delmar Currie Memorial Benefit Golf Tournament. "That first year, our goal was to raise $2,000 for a young boy who has to travel out of country; his family has no assistance with his medical expenses. We raised $4,500 the next year, and guess what, we raised $7,700 the next. I can't wait to work on this benefit tournament next year."

One of the challenges she faces is a tendency to "mother" staff. "I had to learn that's not a good idea," she chuckles, "so I am no longer doing that. Another challenge is keeping up with the accounting/posting part!"

Although there haven't been many "worst" moments, she recalls, "Course marshalling and telling three golfers on a drive car that only two people are allowed on a drive car; only to find out (by them with great grins on their faces) that they owned the car! They were members, it was my first year, and I didn't know them yet. I still die when I think of that and they have fun reminding me of it."

The couple has great plans for the future. "We plan to build a new pro shop in a couple of years and have fun talking with members about it. Also to build two new greens on Holes #12 & #14. Members are going to do a draw on who will get to sit on the bulldozer to tear down the old greens. They are looking forward to that."

Treat your clients/customers the way you want to be treated!

Have notes all over your house/office saying, "When there's a will, there's a way!"

Break rules and make new ones!

Make a budget, make a budget, make a budget!

Strive for progress, not perfection. Don't be too hard on yourself when you make a mistake. Learn from that mistake. Take risks!

Worthy of Note

- Any fall or winter visit to a farmers' market or craft fair will surely reveal someone selling pickles, relishes, or jams. While for most this endeavour is a small one, designed to earn a little extra money, it can be lucrative indeed. Look at Jenny Bick. She never intended to start a pickle company. She and husband, Walter, were Dutch immigrants working the family farm near Scarborough. Ontario. *I Know That Name: The People Behind Canada's Best-Known Brand Names From Elizabeth Arden to Walter Zeller,* by Mark Kearney and Randy Ray, describes how Walter began marketing the pickles Jenny made with a family recipe when they were faced with a huge crop of cucumbers in 1944. The couple, it could be said, struck green gold. The pickles sold so well they focused on growing and pickling cucumbers, opening a small processing plant on the farm and hiring picklers. By 1965, the business had grown and included many types of pickles that were marketed around the world. The Bicks sold out to the company we all know as Robin Hood Multifoods. Not bad for pickles first made in a barn. Too bad the Bick's pickles of today don't reflect the wonderful flavour of those first ones, packed in brine-filled barrels and sold to Toronto-area restaurants, retailers, and army camps.

• Another woman who made an impact on what was to become one of Canada's best-known companies was Charlotte Bowring, also found in Ray and Kearney's *I Know That Name.* Charlotte and her husband, Benjamin, bravely set forth from England to make a new home in St. John's, Newfoundland. Of entrepreneurial bent, the Bowrings, he a watch and clockmaker and she a dry goods merchant, set up businesses side by side in 1811. Charlotte's business was such a success that Benjamin closed down to work with his wife, setting up a retail and importing business that evolved into a thriving department store. The business succeeded, in great part due to Bowring family shipping connections with England. Today, Bowrings are known to us all as wonderful shops to buy household items. Although no longer owned by descendants of the original Bowrings family it remains a privately held, family-owned and -operated Canadian company.

• On a tour of New Brunswick we travelled the back roads to an experience that made for one of the most memorable destinations of the trip. It all started seven years ago at Sainte-Anne-de-Kent, where Isabel P. Gagné created her first batch of pure plant soaps. Today, The Olivier Soapery is a living family country soapery dedicated to the preservation of our Canadian heritage of natural therapeutic treatments, the art of making soap, and the creation of botanical, economical, and ecological skin care products. Isabel (founder, president, derma-specialist, wife, mother, and caregiver of Olivier) and partner Pierre Pelletier (vice-president, marketing manager, father, and care provider of Olivier) have done such a fine job that The Olivier Soapery is one of a small number of Canadian Economuseums. They believe in building long-lasting relationships as part of a big family living, working, thinking, and sharing responsibly. Olivier's mission is "to save the cultural heritage of soap crafting while making an extraordinary life for ourselves, our children, and our customers by providing personalized services that exceed expectations, by pursuing our research and by creating the very best medicinal, botanical, economical and eco-logical skin care products on the planet." Isabel saw the connec-tion between health, beauty, and well-being, and saw the poten-tial for a sustainable family business to help people and the planet. The Olivier Soapery is now a paramedical eco–skin care manufacturer specializing in the creation of the highest quality therapeutic olive oil skin solutions for its customers, its retailers and distributors, and its ambassadors around the world. They give free demonstrations, guided tours of their soap museum, and live interpretation sessions, along with the soap art gallery, soap library, and country soap boutique — ensuring that a visit is an adventure of all the senses!

- Recognized as one of Canada's finest booksellers, McNally Robinson has won the Canadian Bookseller of the Year Libris Award three times in the last ten years. Referring to themselves as a very small "chain" of bookstores, they say the stores are defined by their communities, not by the head office. McNally Robinson operates two stores in Winnipeg, one in Saskatoon, and another in a historic building in downtown Calgary, as well as a library wholesale business in Saskatchewan and Manitoba, Skylight Books. The business, the brainchild of Holly McNally, was started in 1981 with a partner (the Robinson in McNally Robinson). When her former partner left the business, her hus-band, Paul, joined her. The company is an example of how to counteract the often fatal competition that comes to small retail-ers with the invasion of enormous corporate stores. Recognizing the looming threat of big box stores, they decided to beat the American chains by building on their strengths. Most impor-tantly, they remained a regional bookstore featuring local authors and author events, something competitors seldom do. They moved from their small store concept to one that is unique in the industry, expanding to accommodate their growing cus-tomer base. Hosted events are part of the McNally Robinson appeal. The large bookstore includes a full-scale restaurant, yet they are able to keep the small bookstore feel. They remain involved with the community by offering nightly readings and book launches with authors and live music on weekends with local musicians. "Our stores are characterized by warmth, personal service, and local community involvement. We hold hundreds of author events each year, most of them celebrating prairie writers." When they opened the large store they decided that they would not be just a retail outlet but also a cultural centre. It was obviously a wise decision. The couple have grown McNally Robinson from a single store in Winnipeg to a $25-million business, with the second generation, their daughter Tory, now joining the management team. In defining her success, Holly McNally said, in a *Financial Post* profile, "You have to know what you do best and who you really are."

Table Talk Lure to Family Business: Senator Catherine Callbeck

A Prince Edward Islander who joined the family business has gone on to make quite a name for herself. Senator Catherine Callbeck got her first taste of business life at home, for she is one of legions of women who joined a long-established family business. She also represents many Canadian women who parlayed their business experience into a political career.

Vice-chair of the Prime Minister's Task Force on Women Entrepreneurs, she is a strong advocate for WIBs. Her strong, rich voice captivating the audience, she often speaks to gatherings of businesswomen. The occasions typify what this accomplished Islander is: businesswoman, politician, educator, and community activist. Invariably, when introduced, mention is made of the fact that she was Canada's first elected female premier.

Relating her entry into retail, she captures audiences with her insight into the challenges of entrepreneurship and personal memories of finding her place in a family business.

"My grandfather started a business in 1899," she says. "Father took over, then my brother. In 1968 I joined the business."

Originally Callbecks served as tailor shop and store, later evolving into a true general store with an egg grading station and post office. Her initiation began nearby, in the family home. It was in this family business that she first made her mark.

Her formula for success? "You have to have your heart in the business and the business in your heart. It is certainly in mine. I grew up in Central Bedeque. Business was a way of life in our home."

At meal times a young Catherine was all ears as conversation revolved around business, community, and "what was going on." At twelve she began working in the store, continuing through high school and university vacations. She taught business administration for several years, something she "thoroughly enjoyed."

"Once I got into business full-time it swallowed me up very fast," she says, stressing the fulfilment she experienced. "When I came home from Toronto I was fortunate to have the opportunity to become part of the family business," which she describes as, "one stop shopping for building supplies, hardware, carpet, clothing, groceries."

Expanding into furniture, they looked for someone to manage the department.

"We couldn't find an experienced furniture person so I went off to a show to buy furniture. That's how I got started. Didn't know oak from maple," she chuckles. "I took a Bachelor of Commerce and have a Bachelor of Education but you can't learn it all that way, the best education is learned on job. That's basically what I did. I was very much hands on in the operation. We were open six days a week and two nights and I was there most of the time.

"Salesmen would come to me and ask to speak to the furniture manager — never thought I was doing purchasing because I'm a woman. I can give all kinds of examples of that kind of thing, but I never let it bother me. At that time it was rare to be a woman in business."

When their father died his two children assumed management. Under their leadership, Callbeck's Limited of Prince Edward Island continued to evolve. A second furniture store, opened in Charlottetown, became a Leon's franchise.

She credits mentoring with playing an important role in her business career. "My brother has been my mentor. I've been very fortunate in that regard. He is a very astute businessperson."

Her foray into politics brought dramatic change in her focus.

"Senate duties are my priority now. My brother and I rely on people who work for us. We sit down every so often with our managers, look at financial statements and develop strategies and goals. We're involved in all major decisions."

Clothing for Husband Leads to Business: Dawn Griffiths

Dawn Griffiths responded to her husband's diagnosis of malignant melanoma skin cancer by researching and producing sun-protective clothing, and by learning all she could about the disease and what they could do to fight back. As a result, Sun Protective Clothing was formed in 1996 by Dawn and Ron Griffiths. They tell their story on their web site, saying the dangers of ultraviolet radiation from the sun were really revealed when Ron was diagnosed.

"As everyone is aware prolonged exposure to the sun can have serious consequences. Unfortunately most people don't pay attention until they themselves or someone they know is diagnosed with skin cancer. After seeing specialists, Dermatologists and reading everything we could on skin cancer one realizes just how dangerous sun exposure can be. We did not realize that many typical cotton T-shirts and summerweight fabrics can allow 50 percent of harmful UV rays through to your skin when dry and 10–20 percent more when wet. One in seven of our own children now face a risk of getting skin cancer during their lifetime."

They researched and located a summer-weight fabric that provides effective sun protection, brought their background of fifteen years in the garment manufacturing industry to play, and began to produce a line of sun protective casual clothing for the entire family. Their line ranges from men's jackets, sport shirts, and pants to ladies' shirts and pants, from children's shirts and pants and toddler's play suits to a variety of hats for the whole family.

Direct Marketing

The direct marketing method of selling has reached huge proportions, to the point where people become inundated with direct mail, telemarketing, television and radio commercials, catalogues, pop-up screens on web sites, on-line and printed catalogues, even videos and CDs arriving in the mail. So great is the amount of material being flogged that it is acting as a turnoff for many consumers.

This makes putting care and attention into any direct mail campaign a mandatory process. In today's marketplace huge dollars and energy can be wasted on a bad campaign. Yet this is a marketing tool that works well for many businesses. And, as on-line shopping and other high-tech methods gain in popularity, future opportunities for direct marketing look good. Working on the theory that careful planning puts you one step closer to success, consider the following before you start:

- Target your audience, thinking about who they are and how you will approach them. This will influence the style of your presentation and design of promotional and sales materials.
- Collect as much data about potential customers as you can.
- Begin developing a database. You can buy mailing lists, but the most effective are those you compile yourself. Start with former customers. From the beginning set up so that you avoid duplicates. It's annoying to the customer and costly to you. Also include easy address change forms.
- Include demographics in your database. Details like age, gender, location — anything that applies to your product line or service — will be a huge asset as you get into direct mailing.
- Start developing your direct marketing campaign by defining the strong points about your product or service in writing. Include the value it offers to clients, its appeal, how it works, who benefits by acquiring it, and why they should acquire it from you.

- Determine whether you need the help of a professional to design or direct your campaign. You will need strong writing and images — should you hire a writer or photographer? Do you need a graphic designer?

- Before hiring professionals to assist you put down your requirements in writing. Be sure to think through what you can do yourself and detail that as well. You can often cut costs, but only if you are careful in defining the details with those you hire.

- Think about how the potential customer will actually obtain your product: on-line ordering, an order form in a catalogue, a postage pre-paid order card, phone-in orders? Do you take credit cards?

- Before designing any print material get specs from the post office regarding size, weight, and mail preparation procedures. Being a half-inch out, or a gram over weight, can cost mega dollars when doing large mailings. Before actually committing to having material printed, put together a sample mailout — including the envelope. Ask your printer for samples of the paper weights and sizes you are using. Once you have a price from the post office, build in rate increases. We all know the cost of postage goes up almost every year.

- Do you want to go with a personalized approach, actually inserting names into letters? Check out the how-to, and the added cost.

- What about "involvement devices": scratch-off discounts on a card, coupons, that sort of thing. They are good for luring customers in but will affect your profit.

- Whether going for printed material or on-line sales through a web site or e-mail campaign, do make sure that you get several quotes on what it will cost. And ask for detailed quotes that define costs.

- Get others to review your material before going public with it. It's amazing how many typos can slip by, and questions go unanswered. These will hopefully be caught by other sets of eyes.

- Decide how the actual physical mailing will be done. Who will stuff, sort, stick on stamps, do address labels, and handle the physical labour involved in a mailing?
- And finally, who is going to handle the orders and responses that result from your direct marketing campaign? Who is going to update the database to ensure that you serve these new customers well and keep them in the loop for future campaigns?

Chapter Nine:
Meeting the Challenges Head-On

*If you are not having fun, do something different, either
get out or take on something more challenging inside
what you are doing. If you want security, this is not the
world in which you can obtain it ... It is easy to be fearful
but hard to have courage, but you can't be committed to
your fear, so you have no choice but to have courage; you
are remarkable even when you can't see it yourself; what
others are saying is probably true; and at the end of the
day, it is just like anything else in life ... the only thing that
matters is how much you have loved.*
Gretha Rose, Cellar Door Productions

We are all faced with our own unique sets of challenges. I liken them to
the walls in an obstacle course. We have to get to the other side — whether
we go over, around, or blast our way through depends on the unique cir-
cumstance, our personality, and the other factors we have to deal with.

What is important is that we recognize the challenges for what they
are. Not an impenetrable barrier, nor a cell from which there is no
escape, but simply something we have to work around.

For women, challenges range from things medical to things financial, from isolation to family commitments, from butting heads with
the old boys' network to lack of experience and education — the list is
pretty well endless.

Typical of those coping with the isolation challenge was Eleanor
Kennedy, whose tale can be found in *Pioneers and Early Citizens of*

Manitoba, published by Peguis Publishers in Winnipeg. Born in England in 1825, she married a pioneer and explorer of Red River, Manitoba, and the Arctic. A talented painter and musician, she left a legacy of original botanical paintings of Manitoba plants. She taught music and was a leading figure in the settlement of St. Andrew's, where she worked to establish a hospital. The Duchess, as she was known, turned her hand to supporting the family when her husband fell ill. She imported the latest styles from Paris and London, which she sold from a shop on the home property.

The pioneering spirit is, it is obvious, alive and well in Manitoban women, be they early settlers or today's entrepreneurs.

Wildly Successful: Helen Webber and Marie Woolsey

When you consider the experience Marie Woolsey and Helen Webber have at meeting challenges, the idea of starting a business with one part-ner in the far north and the other in Calgary doesn't seem a big deal. In fact, these adventurous gals take the long-distance commute in stride. Consider their backgrounds.

Helen was born in Churchill, Manitoba, to one of the first non-aboriginal families to settle in the area, and she thought the isolation of the community was as rugged as it was going to get. But then along came Doug. He arrived with the Navy, fell in love with the wilderness (and, we presume, Helen), and soon established an air service and an outfitters. With even more isolation in mind, they constructed fly-in lodges: Dymond Lake Hunting Lodge, situated on Hudson Bay, northwest of Churchill, and North Knife Lake Fishing Lodge, in north central Manitoba. Helen has been totally involved in all projects, but her real claim to fame is the incredible meals offered up at one or both of the lodges for over twenty-five years — some-times under primitive and difficult conditions. More recently offer-ing five-star accommodation, they are said to provide the best the North has to offer.

Marie, on the other hand, was plucked out of southern Ontario and dropped into the middle of a native village. Born in Dundas, Ontario, she felt the call of the wild when she married Gary, an Anglican priest-pilot who whisked her off to remote communities in northern Ontario and Manitoba. Very shortly after her move to Churchill, the Webbers and the Woolseys became fast friends, and from this friendship grew Marie's involvement in the lodges. She has been cooking with Helen, part-time, since 1980. Even though she now resides in Calgary, you will find her at the Fishing Lodge every June and at the Hunting Lodge each September. It has always been a team effort — each encouraging the other to experiment with new recipes in order to present their guests with the finest cuisine.

Encouraged by lodge guests to produce a cookbook featuring the wild game they were known for, Helen and Marie formed Blueberries & Polar Bears Publishing in 1994 with the printing of their first cookbook, *Blueberries & Polar Bears*. *Cranberries & Canada Geese* followed, then *Black Currants & Caribou* and *Icebergs & Belugas*. In between, they produced a mini-series of smaller cookbooks: *Wild & Wonderful Blueberries*, *Wild & Wonderful Cranberries*, and *Wild & Wonderful Goose & Game*. After incorporating in 2001, they added to the Wild & Wonderful collection with *Wild & Wonderful Fish* and *Wild & Wonderful Wild Rice*.

Helen Webber and Marie Woolsey have been wildly successful with publications like *Blueberries & Polar Bears;* they divide their time between far north lodges and a Calgary office, for a grand lifestyle.

The colourful books speak of the region they depict, combining tales and stories with good recipes. So, how do they meet the challenge of their geographic locations, of being apart, and of being involved with such intense and distracting work at the lodges? One very important factor that you can immediately recognize when you meet them is that these two women like, respect, and spark each other. Marie and Helen gave us a behind-the-scenes look at life at Blueberries & Polar Bears.

"Our writing is mostly done when we are together. We work best back to back, each with a computer, and a kitchen close by. Our ideas flow much better when we 'chat as we go,'" says Marie. "We have done this at both our homes, at Helen's in-laws, and at the lodges during the season." The travel is something that Helen says was a financial challenge, but worked well.

"At first we didn't know how the business was actually going to be run — it seemed to relate most to the Churchill area — but Helen was already busy with the lodge business, so our office was set up in my home in Calgary. The 800 number reaches me, though most people assume that I am in Churchill," explains Marie.

"Marie does all of the mailing from our home-based office in Calgary as it is much more convenient and more cost-efficient to be doing it from a major centre," adds Helen.

Marie says she had no business experience and precious little natural business sense. "I had to take a bookkeeping course early on in order to prevent the muddle of our first year from being repeated. We each do some book launches and marketing events on our own, but we much prefer to do them together. So we get together at least twice a year, just for marketing events and media trips — which often turn into shopping trips and visiting sessions with friends and relatives," she says.

"It has worked out well for us in a very natural way just as it does when we are working in the kitchen together," says Helen. "We just seem to naturally divvy up the jobs most of the time without even any discussion. We have had observers say that it is just like watching poetry in motion. In fact, it is uncanny how often one of us will make a suggestion about our menu only to discover that the other person has just been thinking the exact same thing.

"One of our challenges was spending a large amount of money to get started. I would never have taken that step on my own. I think we were very presumptuous to think that we could write a cookbook that would sell ten thousand copies — that people would actually enjoy reading and using. We did it without going to any government agency or bank for a loan — we had family that helped us through. Talk about faith! Our first book is now in its fourth printing for a total of forty-five thousand books. The other books just followed naturally.

"The pictures for our first book were taken in a studio in Calgary. We did our best to make them look outdoorsy with fishing tackle and wooden ducks and polar bears and such. But we jokingly said that the pictures for our next book would be taken at the Fishing Lodge in natural surroundings. So, lo and behold, our photographer, Hutch, and his wife, Linda, and our food stylist, Margo, all flew up to North Knife Lake to take the pictures for *Cranberries & Canada Geese*.

"It was the first time they had ever done food pictures out of doors — and what a challenge that was! Each picture was hurriedly taken in spots of sunlight between rainfalls. We only had five days and a maximum of three pictures can be taken on a really good day. If it rained for two or three days, we were in trouble!" she laughs. "But we squeaked through, with great results.

"Naturally, we had to go to another lodge for *Black Currants & Caribou*. We chose Dymond Lake — the goose hunting lodge, on the coast of Hudson Bay. We didn't even wait until the end of the hunting season — so Helen and I were feeding fourteen or fifteen guests, eight or so staff, as well as preparing all the food for the shoots and hosting the photography team.

"Sometimes we would get to eat at the third sitting around nine at night, still having to clean up and then be up again at 4:30. Linda's and Margo's jobs expanded to include dishwashing! And then there was the cold weather. It was September on Hudson Bay — same problem with finding sunny intervals — and if you look at the picture of Helen and me on the back cover, you can see how cold Helen is — I'm a little more hot-blooded.

"So, where would we go for *Icebergs & Belugas*? To Seal River Heritage Lodge, run by Helen's daughter and son-in-law — where ecotourists come to consort with Belugas in the late summer and polar bears in the fall. The weather was much more co-operative this time, but the bugs were ferocious, a couple of polar bears paid us a visit, and in some of our settings we had to contend with tides. Where in the pictures the food is high and dry, an hour later, it would have been under water! But the results, we think, were worth it. We never skimped on our pictures, and we never said, *no*, it can't be done! We were just fortunate that Hutch, Linda, and Margo had an adventuresome spirit that matched our own."

191

Helen, who is, of course, closely aligned to the operation of Webber lodges, said most of the challenges of working in the North relate more to the actual cooking than to working together or forming the company. "Those challenges were mostly due to the distance between us and were greatly lessened with the modern technology that is now available. The biggest challenge my living in the north presented was the cost factor involved when I had to fly to Calgary or Marie had to fly up here.

"As far as our cooking goes, the biggest challenge is getting the fresh produce we need. When you add a 130-mile flight from Thompson to the fishing lodge, to produce that has already traveled from market to Thompson, it can be pretty sad looking when *and if* we get it. When we order, we have no idea if we are going to get everything. When we order something like fresh green beans for example, we have no way of knowing if we will have them until the airplane arrives. It has taught us to be real good at improvising. Likewise, if we have bad weather for a couple of days and our supplies don't get in. Another challenge of the north that is quite unique to Churchill is sharing our berry patches with polar bears and having to be very cautious when we are out picking. We don't leave camp without a radio, scare gun, air horn and a bear dog."

Marie adds, "A lot of people ask whether Helen and I are still good friends. Yes, we are! We still work at the lodges together — smoothly and without tension, and we even holiday together with our husbands. And our business trips? We love them!"

Marie Woolsey says her advice to other women in business would be, "Don't be afraid to ask for advice and help — a lot of people helped us along the way. Fear was probably the biggest obstacle I had to overcome — I had to push myself every step of the way. But the wonderful feeling of having accomplished something new and different and exciting has stretched me and helped me to grow. I am not the same person I used to be — I think that I am more confident and certainly less afraid of the unknown."

Helen encourages women to "take a chance. It is amazing what God can do if we take the first step. Marie and I set out to write one book — *Blueberries & Polar Bears* and here we are nine books later. They should be prepared for hard work and the fact that things will not always run smoothly but if they persevere they can do it! I believe there is a wealth of opportunity out there if we just have the nerve to take that leap of faith. I would also encourage them to talk to people who are involved in similar type ventures. We have found other authors to be very helpful and also in our lodge business, we have received a lot of good advice from other lodge operators. Most people are willing to help!"

Getting the Picture

One of the things that Marie spoke of was the challenges that photography brought to their publishing venture. Not only is it a big financial investment and often very time-consuming, but having the right look in your photos reflects how people see your business; having good images shot can be one of your most important sales, marketing, and promotional tools.

In all things photographic I turn to the family expert, our son, John, who owns and operates Imagemaker Studio in Vancouver. John has photographed a wide range of products and services. His work has appeared in publications around the world, on packaging and album covers, and in numerous promotional mediums. His clients have budgets that range from hundreds to thousands. Bringing a guy into the book isn't really cheating. He and I have a business together that combines my writing and his photography skills. We produce all manner of print material ranging from recipe cards, brochures, and posters to editorial content for books and magazines. John has shot photos for use on billboards, buses, and business cards. We jointly present workshops across Canada with John teaching photography while I focus on writing, publishing, and things relating to small business.

Modern technology allows you to access photographers anywhere — tapping into unique skills and experience. Even though John lives in British Columbia and I'm in Prince Edward Island, he does the majority of our photos, and he doesn't always fly across the country to do it. He sets it up, takes a sample shot, e-mails it, we approve or suggest adjustments. Sometimes that's it. Other times he makes adjustments and then shoots it again. The following advice on getting the photography you need to do the job you need doing is provided by John.

Effective Images Through Detailed Planning: John Watson

In this era of spectacular colour imagery, the old adage "A picture is worth a thousand words" has never been truer. Whether in a brochure, advertisement, catalogue, poster, web site, or through the media, your first point of contact with potential customers is often a photograph.

In our image-based society, visual representation is a vital part of marketing and promotion. If it doesn't grab clients and pull them in, they go on by, because there are hundreds more just a click of the mouse or turn of the page away.

Getting effective images can seem daunting and expensive. The temptation to use snapshots or to "obtain" images from the web or other sources is difficult to resist; however, this is one place where professional expertise pays dividends. There are steps that can be taken to attain effective images, in the correct format, while staying within budget and avoiding pitfalls that can disconcert even the experienced.

Obtaining photographs that do what you want requires careful, detailed planning. One of the most important things to remember is, the more information you have about what you need, the easier it will be to attain. A number of factors should be determined before "leaping in."

What do I need? Determine how the photographs will be used. Contact your creative team (writer, graphic designer, printer, or web designer) to see whether they prefer digital images, transparencies, or prints. Digital photography is common and popular; however, attention to the quality of the image is vital. If using digital images ask the size, file type, dpi, colour mode, etc. If they work from prints they should give you information such as size and finish. Be sure to ask for cost differences between various options and an explanation of how the results will differ. You might not know what all this means, but a photographer does. Determining requirements in advance can save mega dollars.

What will it cost? The key is to decide what you can afford. Be realistic. Fully styled shots with props, complex lighting, and travel to your location will cost more than simple catalogue shots done in a studio. Put your requirements on paper, then approach several photographers for quotes. Have as much information as possible to avoid unexpected costs. Communicate several times with the photographer: for general rates, for a quote when you have a clear idea of what you want to accomplish, and to iron out details. Get an estimate in writing, but remember it is only an estimate. Changes, adding shots, and time delays on the job will all affect the price. Be prepared to pay a deposit.

How do I find a photographer? Word of mouth is the best reference. Ask others with images you admire for a recommendation. Ask your creative team. Check the Yellow Pages. Do a search on the web. Organizations such as the Professional Photographers of Canada and the Canadian Association of Photographers and Illustrators in Communications categorize members by type of work and location.

What am I buying? This is one of the most complex areas of photography. Under law the copyright belongs to the creator unless specified differently. When booking a photographer (or other creators such as writers) ask for their "Terms and Conditions of Ownership and Usage" right up front and make sure you understand exactly what you are buying. That means who owns the photos and how you can use them.

Why pay a pro? When asked why someone should bother hiring a pro, I remind them that a good image tells a story, shows detail, and "sells" for you. A poor one negates quality and suggests you take no pride in what you are trying to sell. It just doesn't make sense to use anything but the best image possible. Professionals study principles of lighting, design, the best ways to produce desired results, effects of various lenses, and so on. Photography can be some of the best, or worst, money spent.

Photography Checklist
Answering these questions helps plan, attain good results, keep control, and budget:

1. How will I use the photographs? On my web site only? In a printed form such as a brochure? How big do I need them to be?
2. What is my budget?
3. How do I want my photo to look? Do I want my product against a plain background (catalogue style)? Do I want to be more creative, adding props to highlight it, or do I want a completely conceptual shot fully styled to simulate use of my product or service?

4. Who is the right photographer?
5. Do I require prints, transparencies, or a digital file? What format: 35mm, 120mm, 4x5?
6. What about copyright and ownership?
7. Where will we take the photos? Photographer's studio? My work area?

Challenges — Medical

Health or medical problems can be one of the biggest challenges any woman will ever face. Whether it is their own health or that of a loved one, it has a huge impact on how women live their lives. In my own life, my husband is a brittle diabetic. While he goes for long periods in relatively good health, he can go down fast and become very ill, often for a week or more. My decision to move out of a downtown office and into home was based, in part, on the need to be nearby during those downtimes. Not only is it better for him to have someone nearby, it also took a huge stress level off my shoulders. Reality is so often far easier to cope with than the imagined!

The increased flexibility allows me to schedule my work around his requirements. Jack took an early retirement for medical reasons and has taken over much of the routine stuff (like washing dishes, cooking, vacuuming, dog walking, and such); however, when he is down I'm there to take over.

The stories of people coping with medical problems are legion, and we are not going to dwell on them because that is a topic for a whole other book. Many, many individuals qualify as genuine heroines for the things they overcome, the positive attitudes they keep, and their achievements. We are just going to take a quick look at how some individuals handle unique challenges. For example, Bev Dolman of Halifax turned the stress of a sleep disorder around. Using the hours when most of us are catching zees to her best interests, she began sewing as a way to pass the time without disturbing her family. Today she owns InVEST In Style, a company we profiled in Chapter 7.

Creating Your Own Niche: Patricia Smith-Matheson

Patricia Smith-Matheson of Edmonton, Alberta, dealt with a double whammy. Her own health has been a challenge of misdiagnosis and difficult to treat disorders. The pain and resulting sleep deprivation can cause a debilitating lack of energy that in turn makes it difficult to function mentally when she is "down." On top of that she took responsibility for her elderly mother-in-law, who needed constant care in her later years. It was not a situation conducive to holding down any job, or even to running most home-based businesses.

When an opportunity to operate a booking service came along, she jumped at it. She began contract work making appointments for a driving school, and later for a janitorial service. The job can be done from home, totally by telephone. When she does have to go out, she takes the cell phones along and stays in control. Today her work has expanded into doing proposals, troubleshooting, writing letters of confirmation, and negotiating contracts.

"Its definitely turned into more than just answering the phone," she says. "It's a neat little business. It could be more lucrative, but I don't have the expenses of clothes, gas, going out to work."

The downside of her work is that it is a seven-day-a-week operation. "When I'm making money on the phone I can't say well, I'm not taking any calls today." The driving school pays her a flat monthly rate for the answering service and a commission for booking courses that range from class one to class six driving instruction. "It's more than booking appointments, this is really sales," she says. "That is how I make my money, by commissions, as well as coordinating and scheduling for the instructors."

With the janitorial service she gets a flat rate for answering the phones as well as a per-call fee. Since she is paid in a manner similar to piecework, taking a day off could well mean a couple hundred dollars in lost income. When working on proposals she charges an hourly rate, and a per page rate for faxes and letters. "Add together and it's a nice little bit of extra money."

She also says she needs to continue working for her own well-being.

"Some days I wonder what am I doing this for, but fact is can't imagine not doing it — at least not right now. The money helps but there is also the feeling of what am I going to do if I don't have it."

On the days when her health problems flare up it is difficult, but she says, "When I'm feeling better I really enjoy it. It has mushroomed into a busy little home-based business. There are not many people around who do what I do and have the experience that I have."

That fact has made her very aware that there are many options open to her in the future.

Flying On Her Own: Rita MacNeil

If there was ever a woman who inspires others it is the gal from Cape Breton who brought us musical affirmation of who we are through songs such as "Flying On Your Own" and "Born A Woman." Her story is an inspiration. This lady is a shining example of the power of believing in yourself, going for it, and doing it your own way. You'll go a long way to find a better role model. Here is her story.

Some time ago in the magical hills of Cape Breton, a very shy girl with a cleft palate knew in her heart that music was everything; it was her dream to write and perform. We know that young girl as Rita MacNeil, a national treasure and an internationally sought after performer. For many of us, her tunes have been an important part of finding ourselves as women.

She grew up in Big Pond, a tight-knit community. In the early 1960s there wasn't much of a music scene in her hometown, so at age seventeen she left to pursue a singing and writing career. It was difficult to leave, especially to leave her mother, who had encouraged her daughter to believe in her dreams. Although she missed her father, a hard-working carpenter and shop owner, and her seven siblings, she stuck it out in Ontario.

"As a single parent to two young children she struggled to support them taking cleaning and waitressing jobs. During the late 60s and early 70s Rita performed at outdoor festivals and smoke filled coffee houses. Lyrical observations, anchored in the growing woman's movement of the day, were embraced by that community, which led to Rita's first record-ing, 'Born A Woman,' in 1975," says her website, www.ritamacneil.com.

In 1978, Rita returned to Cape Breton to perform and discovered an energizing musical community supportive of her music. Rita says, "That's when my career took a better direction. Moving back home, the writing seemed to open up more and I was re-introduced to my roots. My con-nection to other island musicians helped bring everything into focus."

The supportive atmosphere led Rita to the studio for more record-ings. Although there were few production and distribution takers, she independently released "Flying On Your Own" in 1987. The immediate sales and the public response prompted Virgin Records of Canada to champion Rita's musical talent.

When she wasn't in the recording studio, Rita could be found tour-ing Japan, Great Britain, Sweden, Australia, and the U.S. with her band. She was soon found on the stages of Royal Albert Hall in London, England, and the Sydney Opera House in Australia. In Vancouver, dur-ing Expo '86, there was wild enthusiasm for her music.

Recognition of her talents comes from many directions. Rita has received awards and accolades, including being inducted into the Order of Canada. She has produced seventeen albums, live performances, record-ings, and television shows. Although her music reveals some of Rita's innermost reflections on life, her autobiographical book, *On A Personal Note*, reflected the interest in this grand lady, becoming a national best-seller and the basis for a play.

Not all of her endeavours are directly related to her music. During the early touring days, Rita often said from the stage, "If you're ever in Big Pond, drop in for a cup of tea." And they did. If Rita wasn't home, they sometimes left a couple of tea bags in her mailbox. In 1989, the idea for a tea room was born. She renovated an old village schoolhouse, orig-inally purchased as a home, and opened Rita's Tea Room. Nowadays it has expanded, providing many jobs for people in the small community while providing a comfortable stop for tourists and local residents. The tea room includes a gift shop and a Rita memorabilia room, as well as serving baked goods and luncheons.

It's a suitable showcase for the woman who inspired so many women to "fly on their own" and take pride in who and what they are.

Given the challenges Rita faced, she has certainly shown up for her life. As her career grows, not only does the writing flourish, but her ability to see projects relating to her talent also surfaces. You'll go a long way to find a better role model.

Worthy of Note

- *Soho* magazine, in their winter 2004 issue, ran an article called "Determined to Succeed — Resourcefulness, creativity and determination help entrepreneurs with disabilities find success." In it they profiled Paula Crebbin of Oshawa, Ontario, who became the first blind graduate of the Canadian College of Shiatsu Therapy. She now runs her own business, treating about thirty patients, and plans to go back to school to study acupuncture.
- Rebecca Parton, a certified personal trainer, was named a "Soul Model" winner in the March 2003 edition of *Chatelaine* magazine. When Becky, a chronic pain sufferer, was told by a physiotherapist that she was in no shape to take a fitness class, she started her own. Today, this educational assistant at Fort Erie Secondary School in Ontario, who works with kids with a wide variety of disabilities, is helping other women rebound. Her fitness clients range from those recovering from serious injuries or surgeries to those who have suffered a lifetime of physical problems.

Health to Wealth: Vickie Kerr

Two things drove Vickie Kerr into the potato chip business: a desire to make ends meet and a determination to control what her kids ate. Like most moms, she was concerned about junk food. Unlike most people, she didn't just talk about her concerns, she did something about them. The family had a potato farm, so she started experimenting, and after a year she had a snack food that was a hit, Miss Vickie's Potato Chips, cholesterol-free homestyle potato chips for health-conscious consumers.

Getting them to market was a challenge. She needed machines to cut the potatoes and to put the chips into packages. For two years she learned everything she could about the business. Soon they were retailing, and with a third mortgage on the farm, they entered the highly competitive potato chip business. Making the rounds in the farm pick-up truck, she built a market for her chips (which were healthy and tasted better), always asking for, and sometimes getting, cash up front.

When she first opened her business, she had twenty customers. Two years later, her company sold more than $1 million worth of chips as word of mouth increased demand. Sales rose 200 percent by the end of the next year. By 1992 the chips, still hand-stirred while cooking in

Make Choices to Fit Your Plan

Kim Griffin began working in the beverage industry at Labatt Breweries, then spent eight years in the soft drink industry working her way up to national development officer for Pepsi Bottling Group Canada in Toronto. Kim gave up that position to assume a vice-presidency for Ontario for the Brewers of Canada. A supporter of women in business and great motivational speaker, she shares words of wisdom. Kim works with plans and says, "Make sure all of your choices fit your plan, at the same time always be searching for balance. Family is number one in my life, so I make sure that decisions in business fit that." Kim's personal strategy:

- Talk business, it's vital. You need to show you can talk comfortably about strategy in the language of men and your colleagues.
- Know your pillars of strength.
- Have a plan.
- Make choices that fit your plan.
- Know how you will deliver.
- Success in business is about meeting business objectives, making sound business decisions about things that drive the business forward, getting things done that move the company forward.
- And, when it comes to marketing she says, "If you don't have a point of difference on your product you are not going anywhere."

peanut oil in special kettles, were being made in Quebec, British Columbia, and on the home farm in Ontario. The company was sold to Hostess Frito-Lay, leaving the family far better off than when Vickie began making her own chips to save a few pennies, and with much more time to enjoy their family and a new lifestyle.

Brewing Up Business: Susannah Oland and Kazuko Komatsu

A tale from the early days of the brewing biz leads to one of my favourite stories about women entrepreneurs. Susannah Oland began brewing up beer in her Halifax backyard in 1867. The story goes that she brewed a batch of brown October ale that so pleased friends and family that her husband began to market the beer. That first brewery, the Army & Navy Brewery, thrived for several years. Tragedy struck when John Oland was killed in a riding accident, leaving Susannah with seven children to support. She courageously carried on, renaming the brewery S. Oland Sons & Co., an endeavour that prospered until her death in 1886. After her death the "Sons" set out to carry on the family tradition. Since that time, Olands and Moosehead Breweries have flourished, surviving Prohibition, the Depression, and the 1917 Halifax explosion. This endurance is what has made Moosehead Canada's oldest independent brewery, the third largest in the country.

Today another woman is known as a brewer extraordinaire: Kazuko Komatsu, president and CEO of Pacific Western Brewing Company in British Columbia. Western Canada's largest independent Canadian-owned brewery was taken over by Komatsu in 1991. She spent $2.7 million in upgrades, making it the first in North America to achieve ISO 9002 certification. Producing thirteen different types of beers, Pacific Western was also the first Canadian brewery to produce a 100 percent certified organic lager.

As an experienced exporter and supplier of private brand beers, the company earned the distinction of being described as Canada's number-one exporter of beer to Japan, according to the Canada Export supplement "Going Global: Women Entrepreneurs in International Markets from the Department of Foreign Affairs and International Trade," published in

March 2003. Diversifying into export markets was a key component of her plan to turn around the ailing company's fortunes when she took over. With roots in an old sake-brewing family in Japan, she tapped into personal contacts to begin exporting Canadian beer to that market.

Her greatest challenge was penetrating the American market. "The U.S. is a very difficult country to export beer to because there are so many regulations in every state. It's like dealing with fifty countries. In contrast, although Japan has forty-seven prefectures, there is just one set of rules, and no permits are required."

Future plans include yet more export. Having started a joint company in Japan that focuses of health supplements and energy products, Kazuko wants to grow its export sales and diversify product lines by utilizing the unique, pristine water supply exclusive to Pacific Western Brewing. This will entail the manufacturing and distribution of health and energy drinks as well as exclusive bottled water products. They are also looking at researching and developing new BIO products for sale in capsule and beverage format in Canada and abroad.

The future bodes well for this woman who has used a variety of resources to broaden the company's export horizons, including Canada's Trade Commissioners. She participated in the first Canada–U.S. Businesswomen's Trade Mission to Washington in 1997 and has been part of Team Canada trade missions. Attending foreign trade shows brought many new contacts and resulted in her foray into the Chinese market.

Having earned the Order of British Columbia for her accomplishments, as well as a seat on the Team Canada Inc. Advisory Board, she is a strong proponent of business networking and community involvement.

"You must have a quality product or service, and one that is unique from others in the marketplace. Do your research. More than any other country, Canada has a great system of embassies and consulates that can help businesses research and enter foreign markets." She also keeps in constant contact with clients through telephone, e-mail, and visits.

Real Fighter Shines at Newfoundland's Tuckamore: Barb Genge

Ask around for leads on "neat" women to talk to in Newfoundland and you can bet your socks that Barb Genge will be one of the first mentioned. The owner/operator of Tuckamore Lodge, which caters to the outdoor adventure, hunting, and fishing markets, is said to be a powerhouse in the tourism industry. Barb, I was told, is right in the thick of activity, offering remote lodge and winter snowmobiling experiences. She is credited with helping to invent and run the "whole Viking Trail thing," which has proven a very successful tourism initiative. Barb is also a key participant in initiating and managing an environmental project for Eider Ducks. And she's done it all while single-handedly running her operation, successfully, against the odds.

In this chapter on meeting challenges, it is fitting to include Barb Genge because she has addressed and overcome many obstacles — so many that a writer for *Eastern Woods and Water* magazine compared her to the coast region known as Tuckamore, for which her lodge is named.

"Tuckamore is tough," wrote Hugh W. McKervill. "It's a vegetative marvel exemplifying adaptation and the will to survive in the face of hostile environmental conditions. More significantly (although we wouldn't want to press the metaphor too far), tuckamore aptly symbolized the character of this diminutive woman who has not only survived but thrived in an economic environment that can be as unforgiving as the winter winds that whip the northern wilderness."

Since the article, written in 1999, Barb's adventure tours and summer relaxation vacations have "really taken off," she says. "We have been full for the past two years and because of this I am looking to expand here in Main Brook, at another location and in a unique place called Conche which has more history than any other place in Newfoundland Labrador.

"The big draws are: icebergs/whales/puffins/hiking/beaches/space. I'm expanding my present lodge to make the setting for guests more enjoyable. I am also going into bottling water, with three other people, to be sold in the U.S. — Liquid Gold!!"

So what were the obstacles overcome to reach such a promising future? The aspiring outfitter's first challenge was the prevailing attitudes in a male-dominated field. Granted she knew little about "guy things" like shooting, skinning, fishing, or hauling carcasses of moose and such out of the bush. But she learned. And she did have the advantage of knowing about business. She had looked after the financial side of her ex-husband's aviation business. She also knew how to look after folks, having grown up in a home that took in boarders.

Although described as a feminist, she is of the "just get on with it" mentality and doesn't belabour the point. She grew up in the old way, doing chores on the farm, and says her father taught her that you don't get anything worthwhile without hard work. And that is something she is used to.

Early resentment from a community that didn't welcome the idea of outsiders coming in to fish their waters and hunt their lands, and that certainly had no appreciation for the idea of catch and release in order to preserve the resources, made things difficult for a time. The closed-door old boys' network forced her to be "extra good" at what she did. She persevered, doing everything from peddling fish to selling groceries to stay afloat. She even resorted to collecting beer cans and bottles to help pay her bills.

"The hardest challenge was *no* money," she says. "How to get past that hurdle was very stressful, but I know how the homeless survive on what they get that is thrown away ... recycle/reuse is a very real slogan when you are in need of money."

Those hardships were, to a degree, balanced by support from the Departments of Tourism and Fisheries and Oceans, as well as the Atlantic Canada Opportunities Agency, with its interest-free loans. She gives credit to a handful of faithful employees who stuck with her through thick and thin.

Today, regulations aimed to protect resources work in Barb's favour, showing that she was ahead of her time when it came to caring for the environment. As well as hunters and fishers, Tuckamore Lodge offers a total outdoor adventure centre to artists, birdwatchers, photographers, hikers, naturalists — anyone seeking to recharge in the solitude.

In fact, the wonder of the place that keeps her lodges full also serves to keep Barb hooked. When asked why she persevered, she said, "Just to stay in Newfoundland, I didn't fit in Canada before and I am quite sure that I will not now. I like being in business. When I can run out the door when I like, that to me is real freedom."

Barb Genge says accessing assistance has become more difficult. "Government now has young kids working there, and so do banks, who only know numbers and have no social abilities. So, instead of getting easier it is now getting harder to start businesses or expand them ... Be persistent, never give up and stay focused — If I can do it you can do it!! That's my line," says the intrepid entrepreneur.

Lessons in Communication: Nancy Regan

For more than a decade, Nancy Regan communicated with more than a quarter of a million viewers each night as co-host of an hour-long before news television program broadcast throughout Atlantic Canada. In 2003, Nancy signed off to pursue another career in professional speaking. She does a little acting, acts as master of ceremonies, and is seeking new challenges. Nancy says confidence, communication, risk taking, and the art of persuasion are tools we all need to sharpen in order to achieve personal and business excellence. She says the top ten things that TV taught her are lessons in communication:

1. The more you give the more you get.
2. We are all the same — we are all just ordinary people who relate to one another on a human level.
3. You never know what's on the flip side of the pancake — don't let other people's behaviour dictate yours, cut people some slack.
4. It never hurts to ask — the worst that can happen is they say no.
5. Know when to change the channel — to try a different approach.
6. Learn to embrace your inner dork — be able to laugh at yourself.
7. The voices in your head can make you, or break you — if you expect to fail you probably will. If you expect to succeed, you probably will.
8. If you are always afraid to fail ... you'll never succeed — fear of failure is a crippling thing.

9. Being unpredictable can bring predictable results — look for different ways to act that will have positive results.

10. Brains don't belong in boxes — be willing to expand your horizons and look with a new perspective.

Nancy Regan gave up a secure position as a television host to pursue her own business as a professional speaker. The Nova Scotian is a popular motivator for Women in Business.

Culinary Capers Meets the Challenge: Debra Lykkemark

From the day she entered the world of entrepreneurs, Debra Lykkemark, president of Culinary Capers Catering, Party Art Design, Best of the West BBQ, and Culinary Cakes, has faced and overcome obstacles. Nothing, however, prepared her for the most difficult time of her career — the loss of business after September 11.

Back in 1985, she and a couple of friends entered the hospitality business. They couldn't afford the restaurant that Debra dreamed of, so instead they leased and renovated a coffee shop and began doing corporate catering. Looking back, she's glad that she ended up in catering instead of in the restaurant business.

"The catering business has no limits to the type of food or number of guests you can serve. It is very challenging as you are constantly working in new environments with new concepts."

Working as a waitress and bartending in a Calgary restaurant had given her a background, but when she moved to Vancouver in 1980 she was amazed by the cuisine being served. "I decided to go to Debrulle Culinary School." After graduation she was an apprentice chef for a year and spent a year at the Pan Pacific Hotel before starting the business.

Debra Lykkemark faced down the challenges to become one of Vancouver's top caterers. Party Art design, Culinary Capers, and sister companies lead the market in entertaining.

"The first five years were very tough. We were operating on a shoestring and didn't have the extra money for marketing." They outgrew the coffee shop kitchen and so leased a second commercial kitchen while still operating the coffee shop. "My partners decided they wanted out in the fourth year of business, as we still weren't making a profit I was able to buy them out for their original investment."

Her husband, Michael Harris, joined the company in 1991 and adopted the challenge of marketing. He took the company from sales of $500,000 in 1991 to just under $4 million in 2001. He remains in charge of marketing and oversees purchasing, equipment, and facility management. She also has great staff.

"My secret to success is surrounding myself with positive people. Good people attract other good people until you have created a culture that thrives on positive energy. I believe in hiring people that are strong where you are weak and delegating responsibility to my management team. If you want your company to grown and prosper you cannot do it all yourself."

In the aftermath of September 11, large parties from conventions and incentive travel disappeared as groups downsized, cancelled, or switched to locations closer to their homes. Businesses tightened their belts, cutting back on corporate catering and Christmas parties.

"For the first time I had to manage a shrinking company. Fortunately we acted quickly, many companies did not, hoping that the economy would spring back. We went from $3.9 to $3.2 million in sales. In order to remain profitable it was necessary to trim $30,000 off expenses each month. The first thing we did was renegotiate all our contracts, i.e. rent, insurance, yellow pages, health plan. We stopped spending in any area that did not directly affect the quality of our customer service or product. We still had to make further cuts, which involved laying off some of our staff. This was a very difficult thing to do, but was absolutely necessary to keep the company healthy."

Debra says business slowly returned to the volume of sales pre–September 11. "I carefully add staff as the need arises. My long-term plan is to continue to grow the catering and the decor division of the company, Party Art Design."

Training and ongoing education is the key to being a market leader in the catering industry, and all Culinary Capers staff are encouraged and expected to not only attend but also participate in special event and catering conferences by offering their expertise as panel members or featured speakers.

"By sponsoring our staff at these events we are able to spot trends, brainstorm with colleagues from all over North America, and stay on the leading edge of new ideas and innovative presentations for cuisine and decor," says Lykkemark, who recently served a two-year term as the president of the International Caterers Association.

The range of awards and extravaganza events catered is far too numerous to list here. Perhaps the most memorable was catering for 4,500 guests at an NHL All-Star Gala in Vancouver. The 168 staff for the evening consisted of 58 bartenders, 30 chefs, 70 waiters, 10 supervisors, and 20 coat check attendants. Staff served 2,520 oysters on the half shell, 4,500 pieces of sushi, 12,000 hors d'oeuvre, 8,000 dim sum dumplings, 300 pounds of salmon, and 600 pounds of ham, beef, and turkey. Their designers installed themed decor for 15 food stations, and 15 bars consumed 4,000 pounds of ice.

She plans to have a strong young management team in place so she can take more time off. She is looking ahead to the Winter Olympics and the business she anticipates from that event.

Debra Lykkemark has five top tips for women entrepreneurs:

- Love what you do.
- Surround yourself with positive people, in and outside of work.
- Determination and focus are key to success.
- Hire people who are strong where you are weak.
- Delegate by finding the right management team and then empower them.

It's All About Life

I was within forty-eight hours of sending away the manuscript for this book when I decided to take a couple of hours to relax — the idea was to go away, have a gab with friends, and come back feeling all refreshed and full of creative energy.

So there I was at a breakfast meeting of the Prince Edward Island Business Women's Association. The meeting was organized so that a number of members did a short presentation on who and what they are. Excellent networking! The last of these business presentations was by Debby Beck, owner of Montague Computer! in Montague, P.E.I., a long-time supporter of WIB activities.

Debby stood behind a table and whipped the covering from a cardboard box. Rummaging inside she brought out a clear plastic container — sort of like a square-edged, over-large vase. She began filling the container with golf balls. Once they were to the brim she asked the audience if the jar was full. Many agreed that, yes, it was.

So Debby pulled out small pebbles, shaking the container as she poured them in. The pebbles rolled into the open areas between the golf balls. She asked, "Is the jar full?" Again, many agreed that yes, now it was.

She next pulled out fine sand. Of course, the sand filled up every remaining space. She again asked, "Is the jar full?" The "yes" was now unanimous.

Debby produced a bottle of wine and poured it into the jar, effectively filling any empty space left by the sand.

"Now," she said, as the laughter subsided, "I want you to recognize that this jar represents your life. The golf balls are the most important things — your family, your children, your health, your friends, your favourite passions — things that if everything else was lost and only they remained would ensure your life will still be full.

"The pebbles are the other things that matter, like your job or business, your house, your car. The sand is everything else — the small stuff.

"If you put the sand into the jar first, there is no room for the pebbles or the golf balls. The same goes for life. If you spend all your time and energy on the small stuff, you will never have room for the things that are important to you. Pay attention to the things that are critical to your happiness. Play with your children. Take time to get medical checkups. Take your significant other out to dinner. Play another eighteen holes of golf. There will always be time to clean the house and bake a cake.

"Take care of the golf balls first, the things that really matter. Set your priorities. The rest is just sand."

Someone in the audience raised her hand and inquired what the wine represented. Debby smiled. "I'm glad you asked. It just goes to show you that no matter how full your life may seem, there's always room for a bottle of wine!"

I can't think of a better way to end this book. Remember the plan. It's all about putting the things that *really* matter first.

Index

Getting in Touch

T.Allen & Associates, Inc. (page 115)
PO Box 293, Charlottetown, PE, C1A 7K4
1-866-628-1140 Fax: 902-892-1098
tracey@tallenassociates.comwww.tallenassociates.com

ARK BioMedical Canada Corp. (page 171)
Marjorie E. Stevenson-Dawson
902-892-5244
www.arkbio.ca

Blueberries & Polar Bears Publishing Inc.
(page 188)
Helen Webber and Marie Woolsey
184 Cedar Ridge Cres., S.W.
Calgary, AB, T2W 1X8
1-800-490-2228
mwoolsey@bbpbcookbooks.com
www.bbpbcookbooks.com

Senator Catherine Callbeck (page 14, 181)
Prime Ministers Task Force on Women
Entrepreneurs
Room 354, East Block
Ottawa, ON, K1A 0A4
1-800-267-7362

Anne Chouinard (page 45)
c/o Canadian Golf Academy
P.O. Box 1359
Montague, PE, C0A 1R0
1-888-698-4653
achouinard@canadiangolfacademy.ca

Cellar Door Productions Inc. (page 73)
Gretha Rose, President
90 University Ave., Suite 406
Charlottetown, PE, C1A 4K9
902-628-3880

www.cellardoor.tv

Cloverdale Reporter News (page 138)
Ursula Maxwell-Lewis, Publisher & Managing
Editor
17586-56A Ave.
Cloverdale, BC, V3S 1G3P
604-575-2405
crnews@shaw.cawww.CloverdaleReporter.com

Creative Esthetics Dental Lab Inc. (page 71)
Cathy Rose, President
94 Watts Avenue, West Royalty Industrial Park
Charlottetown, PE, C1E 2C1
902-566-5313
www.ubfi@creative-esthetics-dental-lab.com

Cuisine "Dina" (page 140)
Dina Sippley
Moncton, NB
506-389-3994

Culinary Capers Catering (page 207)
Debra Lykkemark
Vancouver, BC
604-875-0123
www.culinarycapers.com

DLO Move Support Services Ltd. (page 173)
Donna Oseen
1264 West 21st St.
North Vancouver, BC, V7P 2C9
604 990-0135
admin@dlo.ca
www.dlo.ca

Devlin Ink (page 111)
Sandra Devlin
81 Weston St.

Moncton, NB, E1A 7B8
506-384-4770
sdevlin4770@rogers.com

Dmajor Fabric Studio Ltd. (page 156)
Doreen Smith and Chum Lootsma
545 Malpeque Rd.
Winsloe, PE, C1E 1Z2
902-368-1056

Dog Paddling Adventures (page 54, 165)
Kathryn Howell
177 Idema Road
Markham, ON, L3R 1A9
905-477-2493
jessie@dogpaddlingadventures.com

Down-To-Earth Creations (page 148)
Maria "Maia" Heissler
259 Maybee Rd., R. R. # 1,
Frankford, Ontario K0K 2C0
613-398-6703
maiasforestfriends@sympatico.ca

Fairwind Embroidery (page 164)
9 Trinity Street
St. John's, NF, A1E 2M3
709-579-4834
the.tuckers@nf.sympatico.ca

Sandra Field, author (page 96)
www.eHarlequin.com

Debbie Gamble-Arsenault (page 117)
1320 Pownal Road
R.R. #1, Alexandra,
Charlottetown, PE, C1A 7J6
902-569-3913
dgamble@isn.net
www.isn.net/~dgamble

Get Organized for Success Ltd. (page 123)
Tami Reilly
North Vancouver, BC
604-903-2120, Fax: 604-990-0961
info@gogetorganized.com

Glen Afton Golf Club (47, 176)
Merina Currie
Nine Mile Creek, P.O. Box 235
Cornwall, PE, C0A 1H0
1-866-675-3001
www.glenaftongolf.com

Cheryll Gillespie (page 101, 128)
52nd Street

Edmonton, AB, T5A 0B6
Fax: 780-473-5013
cg@cheryllgillespie.com
www.cheryllgillespie.com/meetcheryll.htm

Michelle Grant (page 118)
www.telusplanet.net/public/mmgrant.index.html

Kim Griffin (page 201)
Brewers of Canada
www.brewers.ca

Guild Hall Productions (page 127)
Maureen Saumer, Agent
P.O. Box 72097
Edmonton, AB, T6B 3A7
780-944-9504

Marjorie Harris (page 87)
garden writer
http://www.marjorieharris.com

Hearts Ease Creations (page 152)
Wendy Alkins Pobjoy
902 659-2263
wendy@heartsease.ca
www.heartsease.ca

Bobbi Hutchinson (page 95)
www.eHarlequin.com

InVEST In Style (page 145)
Bev Doman
84 Briarlynn Cres
Dartmouth, NS, B2V 1K6
902-434-0814

Island Tee Times & Travel (page 47)
Maureen Kerr and Amanda Stewart
Shops at St. Avards, 8 Mount Edward Rd.
Charlottetown, PE, C1A 5R8
1-877-464-6535, Fax: 902 367-4832
www.islandteetimes.com

Kilmalu Farms Daylily Nursery (page 109)
Suzanne Johnston
624 Kilmalu Road RR#2
Mill Bay, BC, V0R 2P0
250-743-5446
www.kilmalu.com

La Tranchefile (page 152)
Odette Drapeau, Isabelle Chasse
5251 Saint-Laurent Blvd.
Montreal, PQ, H2T 1S4
514-270-9313

reliure@latranchefile.com
www.latranchefile.com

Last Mountain Lake Apiaries (page 118)
Jean Fletcher
Jean's Skin Cream
765 Royal St.
Regina, SK, S4T 4Z3
306-545-1349

Life Design Unlimited (page 82)
Lekha Shah
250 472-8964
www.lifedesignunlimited.com

Patricia Lovet-Reid (page 175)
c/o Key Porter Books
416-862-7777

Rita MacNeil (page 198)
www.ritamacneil.com

Linda MacPhee (page160)
MacPhee Workshops
www.macpheeworkshop.com/patfab.html

McNally Robinson Booksellers (page 180)
www.mcnallyrobinson.com

Montague Computer (page 210)
Debby Beck
902 838-2430
debby@mci97.com
www.mci97.com

Muttluks Inc. (page 53)
Marianne Bertrand
301 Danforth Rd.
Toronto, ON, M1L 3X2
1-888-MUTTLUK (688-8585)
muttluks@muttluks.com

New Life Products (page 130)
Mrs. Verna Becker, Distributor
14924 69 St. NW,
Edmonton, AB, T5C 0J1
780-475-4507

OCEANS Ltd. (page 62)
Judith Bobbitt, M.Sc., President
65A LeMarchant Road
St. John's, NL, A1C 2G9
709 753-5788
www.oceans.nf.net

Olivier Soapery (page 179)

Isabel Gangé
831 Route 505
Ste-Anne-de-Kent, NB, E4S 1J9
1-888-775-5550

Pacific Western Brewing Company (page 202)
Kazuko Komatsu
Burnaby, BC
www.pwbrewing.com

Page One Productions Inc. and Mail Order
Mama (page 80, 91)
Ann Douglas, author
3108 Frances Stewart Road
Peterborough, ON
705-742-3265
www.having-a-baby.comwww.mailorderma-
ma.com

Prime Ministers Task Force on Women
Entrepreneurs (page 14, 181)
Senator Catherine Callbeck
Room 354, East Block
Ottawa, ON, K1A 0A4
1-800-267-7362

Sabina Hill Northwest Coast Design (page 161)
Sabina Hill
205-1445 West 13th Avenue
Vancouver, BC, V6H 1P2
604 736-3034
www.sabinahill.com

Sandra Phinney (page 98)
P.O. Box 28
Yarmouth, NS, B5A 4B1
902 648-0462
s.phinney@ns.sympatico.ca
www3.ns.sympatico.ca/s.phinney/

Prince Edward Island Specialty Chip Company
(page 120)
Dorece MacMillan, owner/operator
R.R. #3, Marshfield,
Charlottetown PE, C1A 7J7
902-629-1818
peichips@hotmail.com

Prince Edward Island Spice Merchants (page 76)
Karen Murray
P.O. Box 693
Charlottetown, PE, C1A 7L3
902 569-1770, Fax: 902 569-1798
peispice@isn.net

The Rat Works (page 133)

Sylvia Ross
818 Ski Club Road,
North Bay, ON, P1B 8E5
ratworks98@hotmail.com
705-472-6115

Nancy Reagan Inc. (page 206)
www.nancyreagan.ca

Simon Teakettle Ink (page 80, 89)
Barbara Florio Graham
535 Charles-Desnoyers
Gatineau, QC, J8P 3X4
819-663-3206
simon@storm.ca www.SimonTeakettle.com

Sun Protective Clothing Ltd. (page 183)
Dawn Griffin
598 Norris Court
Kingston, ON, K7P 2R9
613-384-3230, Toll-free: 1-800-353-8778, Fax:
613-384-2780
sunprotection@sympatico.ca

The Bargains Group (page 60)
Jody Steinhauer
890 Caledonia Road
Toronto, ON, M6B 3Y1
416-785-5655
www.bargainsgroup.com

Tuckamore Lodge (page 204)
Barb Genge

P.O. Box 100
Main Brook, NF, A0K 3N0
709.865.6361, Fax: 709.865.2112
www.tuckamore-lodge.nf.net

Julie Watson (page 27)
Creative Connections and Seacroft
P.O. Box 1204
Charlottetown, PE, C1A 7M8
902-566-9748
julie@gotocreativeconnections.com
www.gotocreativeconnections.com

Kasey Wilson (page 66)
kasey@telus.net

Windy Hollow Stoneware (page 55)
Margaret L. Sawyer
110 Albert Mines Rd.,
Edgetts Landing, NB, E4H 151
506-734-2060

Woodleigh Replicas & Gardens (page 169)
Linda P. Steele, Owner
R.R. #2
Kensington, PE, C0B 1M0
902 836-3401
www.woodleighreplicas.com

Zinter Brown Taste Treats (page 36, 56)
Joanne Zinter
780-487-9334
www.zinterbrown.ab.ca

Recommended Reading

Financial Strategies for Women
Shirley D. Neal, Sherrye E. Emery, Jacquelin A. Papke
W.I.N. (Women's Investment Network) Inc.
ISBN: 0-9698065-0-7
A step-by-step guide to a basic financial plan for everyone. Sound ideas to save money, make informed financial decisions, and plan for a secure retirement.

How to Reduce the Tax You Pay
Key Porter Books
ISBN: 1-55263-258-X
Easy to read guide to tax planning, revised regularly to keep it current.

I Know That Name! The People Behind Canada's Best-Known Brand Names From Elizabeth Arden to Walter Zeller
Mark Kearney and Randy Ray
Hounslow, The Dundurn Group
ISBN: 1-5502-407-8

Meaningful Marketing
Doug Hall
Brain Brew Books
ISBN: 1-55870-681-X
"100 Data-Proven Truths and 402 Practical Ideas for Selling More with Less Effort." A well-researched, well-written, reader-friendly book filled with practical, actionable ideas.

Rich Is a State of Mind: Building Wealth and Happiness — A Blueprint
Robert Gignac and Michael Townshend
Taynac & Associates
ISBN: 0-9731849-0-6
available at www.richisastateofmind.com
Dozens of books tackle the subject of personal finance, most of them dry and stodgy. Not this one. From the moment you begin to read you are drawn into the tale of a slightly dysfunctional Canadian family. It's a well-rounded presentation that uses exceptional storytelling abilities to explore managing your finances in a very humanized way.

Roughing it In the Market: A Survival Toolkit for the Savvy Writer
Angie Gallop
Periodical Writers Association of Canada
ISBN: 0-9694028-1-3

This is a terrific little book chock-full of real information. It should be emulated by other professional organizations. Gallup presents practical tools and encouragement from Canadian freelance writers who have been successfully making a living; provides how much to charge, checklists to help you create estimates, sample letters, a sample contract, and advice on negotiating. It is directed to writers, but any businessperson will benefit by reading it, particularly those doing freelance or contract work.

Sanity Savers: The Canadian Working Woman's Guide to Almost Having it ALL
Ann Douglas
McGraw-Hill Ryerson Limited
ISBN: 0-07-560539-2
A smorgasbord of innovative solutions, along with a healthy dose of humour, for the millions of Canadian working women struggling to balance competing demands of work and personal life. One of Canada's most prolific writers, Douglas approached her subject matter with zeal, identifying key areas of stress and giving workable solutions to balance home, work, love, and life! Topics include: winning at office parties, parenting in the express line, juggling your priorities at work, when worlds, collide and even flying solo (is self-employment the answer?).

Surprise! You're Wealthy: A Woman's Guide to Protecting Her Wealth
Patricia Lovett-Reid
Key Porter Books
ISBN: 1-55263-467-1
Addresses financial planning needs of women; the book title reflects the ways in which may women come into money — through a crisis: the death of a family member or a divorce. The book is written to encourage women to identify and create action plans around quantifiable investment goals. "In my experience," says the author, "it's neglect that leads people astray. Procrastination is one of the biggest obstacles to financial well-being."

Information Sources

There are dozens of support associations for women entrepreneurs. Networking and educational groups have formed to serve a wide variety of needs. The best way to find one that suits your needs is through word of mouth. Web searches will turn up a proliferation of groups. Also check your local government offices and ask for referrals. It's simply a matter of finding the groups that suit your needs. The following is a just a sample of what is available.

Women

Aboriginal Women in Business
www.aboriginalcanada.gc.ca; also www.aboriginalcanada.gc.ca/abdt/interface/interface2.nsf/eng-doc/0.html

Alberta Women's Enterprise Initiative Association
www.awei.ab.ca

Association of Women Business Owners of the Lower Mainland BCP
604-878-6699
info@wbo.ca

Business and Professional Women
(The Canadian Federation of Business and Professional Women's Clubs, better known as BPW Canada)
www.bpwcanada.com

Business Women In Trade
www.infoexport.gc.ca/businesswomen/menu-f.asp

Canadian Association of Women Executives and Entrepreneurs
http://www.cawee.net

Canadian Research Institute for the Advancement of Women
www.criaw-icref.ca

Canadian Women's Business Network
www.cdnbizwomen.com

Canadian Woman Entrepreneur of the Year Awards
www.cweya.com

Centre for Women in Business
Mount Saint Vincent University
416-929-7654
www.msvu.ca/cwb

Newfoundland and Labrador Organization of Women Entrepreneurs (NLOWE)
709-754-5555
www.nlowe.org

Prince Edward Island Business Women's Association
902-892-6040
www.peibwa.org/index.asp

RBC Royal Bank — Women Entrepreneurs
www.royalbank.com/sme/women

Reseai des femmes d'affaires du Quebec
www.rfaq.ca

Women Business Owners of Manitoba-Winnipeg
www.wborn.mb.ca

Women in Business Initiative
Atlantic Canada Opportunities Agency
506-851-2271
www.acoa-apeca.gc.ca

Women Empowering Women
www.womenempoweringwomen.biz

Women Entrepreneurs of Canada
www.wec.ca

Women's Enterprise Initiatives:
Alberta: www.aweia.ab.ca
British Columbia: www.wes.bc.ca
Manitoba: www.wecm.ca

Women Entrepreneurs of Saskatchewan Inc.
306-477-7173
www.womenentrepreneurs.sk.ca

Women's Executive Network
416-361-1475, ext. 224

General Business

Canada Business Services Centres
www.cbsc.org

Exporting

Department of Foreign Affairs and International Trade
1-800-267-8376

221

www.dfait-maeci.gc.ca

Intellectual Property

The Canadian Intellectual Property Office,
Industry Canada
info.ic.gc/ca/opengov/cipo
819-953-7620

Travel

The North American Travel Journalist Association selected Journeywoman.com as Best Online Travel Magazine. They have two sites:
Connecting women travellers worldwide, www.journeywoman.comHERmail.net
Women's International Travel Directory, www.HERmail.net

About the Author

In 1983, with several years working for a newspaper and magazine under her belt, Julie V. Watson knew that she wanted to be more independent, to move up her career ladder, and to see the results of her labours impacting her bank account, instead of an employer's.

She also knew that to succeed in her chosen career as a freelance writer and author, she had to do two things. She needed to treat writing as her business. And she had to have a plan that kept her on track and focused on defined goals. She also knew that her family, her husband and son, always had to be her first consideration when it came to making decisions.

Now, some twenty years later, Julie is the author of seventeen books and hundreds of magazine articles, published around the world. She owns two businesses. Although she primarily writes books and articles under her own name, Creative Connections acts as an umbrella business that she uses for commercial clients. "Basically we connect uniquely skilled people as needed," she explains. "A project such as production of promotional press kits or print material might require a photographer, designer, printer, proofreader, and of course the writer and team coordinator. I sub-contract what is needed — thus the 'creative connection.'"

Her second business, Seacroft, focuses on publishing and marketing. Publishing projects range from a family cookbook for a client to *Motorcycle Prince Edward Island*, an annual guidebook, to a series of greeting cards and other gift items for retail sale. Seacroft, a partnership with her husband, also markets her books and family crafts through mail order and craft fairs.

Julie has long been a supporter of women seeking self-sufficiency and fulfillment through entrepreneurship. She served as a board member with the Atlantic Women Business Owners Association, before leaving to help establish a

Prince Edward Island chapter. Later, she was part of a team that brought rebirth to the WBA support group as the Prince Edward Island Business Women's Association. Julie acted as a judge for entrepreneur awards for several consecutive years and has filled the same role for the writing and culinary communities. She is also an active member of the Periodical Writers Association of Canada, Travel Media Association of Canada, Cuisine Canada, and Prince Edward Island Motorcycle Touring Club.

She is a firm believer in the importance of planning doable steps to attain success, of networking, and of women supporting women. She gives back to the community that supports her by sharing knowledge and enthusiasm. Today she not only writes, she is also a busy workshop leader and presenter, passing along her skills to aspiring and established entrepreneurs, as well as writers. She is devoted to her husband, Jack, her photographer son, John, his wife, Chrissy, her parents, and Tipsy, the mini-schnauzer who really calls the shots.

Julie has been the recipient of several awards through her career, including the Gold 2003 Canadian Food Culture Award presented by Cuisine Canada and the University of Guelph, and the 2004 Media Award presented by the Tourism Industry Association of Prince Edward Island.

Julie loves to hear from her readers. Contact her at julie@gotocreativecon-nections.com or through her website, www.gotocreativeconnections.com.

"The dream is the beginning of the journey. The plan and action are what get you to the destination."